Working in the Bathtub

Conversations with
the Immortal
Dany Laferrière

Working in the Bathtub

Conversations with the Immortal Dany Laferrière

ADAM LEITH GOLLNER

Cover design by Debbie Geltner
Book design by Tika eBooks
Proofreading by Jennifer McMorran
Cover photo copyright © *La Tribune* / Jessica Garneau.
Author photo copyright © Michael James O'Brien.

Printed and bound in Canada.

Library and Archives Canada Cataloguing in Publication

Title: Working in the bathtub : conversations with the immortal Dany Laferrière / by Adam Leith Gollner.
Names: Gollner, Adam, 1976- author, interviewer. | Laferrière, Dany, interviewee.
Identifiers: Canadiana (print) 20200210424 | Canadiana (ebook) 20200210467 | ISBN 9781773900735 (softcover) | ISBN 9781773900742 (EPUB) | ISBN 9781773900759 (Kindle) | ISBN 9781773900766 (PDF)
Subjects: LCSH: Laferrière, Dany—Interviews. | CSH: Authors, Canadian (French)—Interviews. | LCGFT: Interviews.
Classification: LCC PS8573.A348 Z643 2020 | DDC C843/.54—dc23

The publisher gratefully acknowledges the support of the Government of Canada through the Canada Council for the Arts, the Canada Book Fund, and Livres Canada Books, and of the Government of Quebec through the Société de développement des entreprises culturelles (SODEC).

Linda Leith Publishing
Montreal
www.lindaleith.com

À n'importe ce qui valut
Le blanc souci de notre toile.

—Stéphane Mallarmé, *Salut*

Table of Contents

INTRODUCTION
THE STORY OF EVERYONE
EVERYWHERE

Dany Laferrière was born in Port-au-Prince in 1953. His father, a former mayor of the city, was forced into exile by François "Papa Doc" Duvalier in 1959. For the next five years, young Dany lived with his grandmother Da in the coastal village of Petit-Goâve, where his aunt Renée was the local librarian. Then, when the time came for middle school, he returned to the capital and his mother, who worked as an archivist for City Hall. He eventually became a culture reporter at *Le Nouvelliste, Le Petit samedi soir,* and Radio Haiti-Inter. At the age of 23, after the assassination of his best friend and close colleague, journalist Gasner Raymond, he fled the country.

Laferrière arrived in Montreal as the 1976 Olympics were getting underway. He found a way to survive on odd jobs (some very odd) and began writing fiction while living in the city's Quartier Latin. His first book, set in carré Saint-Louis during the sticky heat of summertime, was *How to Make Love to a Negro Without Getting Tired* (1985). An immediate success, it established a penchant for memorable titles. And like many of his subsequent works, the book tells the story of a writer writing a story that ends up being the book the reader is reading.

From 1990 until 2002, Laferrière and his family resided in Miami, where he completed ten books. Moving back to Montreal, he reached his widest audience with his 18th novel, *The Return* (2009), winner of the Prix Médicis. Written in a mixture of verse and prose, it's ostensibly about a son returning his deceased father's remains to the Haitian homeland they've both been exiled from. Beyond the subject matter, it, too, belongs to the same singular category that all his books fit into. Each is about a period in his life; each touches on and connects to other periods and other books; and each seems to constantly be on the verge of becoming something else altogether, the sculptural facade not simply cracking apart but the powder of its marble core drifting gently along a breeze into some ululating sunset. Most of the books are, at the same time, about writing and reading and art.

His oeuvre, presently over 30 volumes, is one long interconnected book about his writing of that book. He calls the entirety of his collection *An American Autobiography.* "I like it when things don't have a beginning or an end," he says, in what could pass for a mission statement. There's something Proustian and Faulkneresque about this endeavour, but Laferrière's Caribbean-Québécois Yoknapatawpha *perdu* is as postmodern as it is electrifying.

Some of his books are more about Haiti: *Down Among the Dead Men* (1997), *Le cri des oiseaux fous*[1] (*The Cry of Mad Birds*, 2000), *The World is Moving Around Me* (2013). These centre on his family home, on childhood and adolescence, on life under a dictatorship, on the realities of life in Haiti today. Others are, to a greater extent, Montreal-based: *A Drifting Year* (1994), *Eroshima* (1987), and that sensational debut, *How to Make Love to a Negro Without Getting Tired.* A number of his texts bind Haiti to Montreal, the harshness of a snowbound northern island blending into the sunny noise of the tropics, where "night be-

---

1   French titles are used for Laferrière's books not yet published in English, with their translated meanings in parentheses.

comes a Chagall painting."

He has also written several genre-confounding books that could be classified as un-self-help. His essay collection *L'art presque perdu de ne rien faire* (*The Almost Forgotten Art of Doing Nothing*, 2011) is, he explains, an autobiography of his emotions. (Then again, he has said the same thing about all of his other books.) A recent work, *Tout ce qu'on ne te dira pas, Mongo* (*Everything They Won't Tell You, Mongo*, 2015), is a kind of guidebook for newly arrived immigrants to the first world. The author of three children's books and three illustrated novels, he has additionally been a screenwriter (2005's *Heading South* stars Charlotte Rampling) and directed a film, *How to Conquer America in One Night* (2004). "I think you can do many things as a writer, so I do," he says.

His delightful *Journal d'un écrivain en pyjama* (*Journal of a Writer in Pyjamas*, 2013) consists of 202 short instructional passages on being an author. What does he say it takes to write a novel? A sturdy pair of buttocks; three years of anguish; a few days of partying; plus the ability to change into a plant or a stone. What else? A writer should live in a city they don't like, so they can write all day without feeling like they are missing out on anything. A writer should be a sorcerer who spills their spells, a trapeze acrobat who doesn't freak the audience out too much, a bongo player who lives to play the bongos. A writer should inject a short sentence between longer ones, for rhythm. A writer should focus on immortal themes: ideally love, or death, but in a sly way, as though withholding a secret.

Laferrière is currently a sitting member of the Académie Française, the highest honour a francophone writer can receive after the Nobel Prize. Members of the Académie are known as the "immortals." Following tradition, he inherited his chair from previous members; *fauteuil* number two was held in the past by the likes of Montesquieu (1689-1755) and Alexandre Dumas *fils* (1824-1895). As is customary with all new members, the Académie Française also bestowed one word on him, which is to be *his* word. That word is *valiant*. "To be courageous," he says, "is to act in reality the way you would have in a dream."

A taxi driver in Port-au-Prince once told me that he felt that Dany Laferrière's story was every Haitian's story. To me, his story feels like it could be the story of every Montrealer. His novel *I Am a Japanese Writer* (2008) suggests that his story may actually be the story of everyone everywhere. "I'm from the country of my readers," he explains. "When a Japanese person reads me, I become a Japanese writer."

The precise way he goes about erasing borders is a mystery, perhaps even to him. That's part of the reason I wanted to interview him. Could it have something to do with how his narratives reconfigure memories within observations and reveries, often in a highly romanticized manner? Is it the way he channels sense-based data and details onto the page? What makes the images detonate so vividly in our hearts? "The books are simultaneously my actual life and my dream life," he offers. "I see no distinction between writing and real life."

His narrators are always a version of himself. They're sometimes unnamed, sometimes called Man, or Vieux, or Old Bones—or Laferrière. As he likes to say, he writes the way he lives. And all of his works meander along alluring paths and tangents, so the reader never quite knows where it is all leading. Something as seemingly straightforward as a meditation on the patience and perseverance required of writers inevitably threatens to morph into a rock opera concept album with tracks about how the protagonist's life resembles Modigliani's.

He accepts that the word *flou* (blurred, vague, unclear) applies. He considers haziness an essential component of his writing. And, as I learned, he not only writes the way he lives—he also talks that way. During our interviews, he was quick to contradict himself as need be, starting answers by saying "Yes, no" or "No—yes." The ambiguity about what's true and what isn't, and the impossibility of defining him with any finality, is part of the fun of reading him. He'll drop a line about "my friend Saul Bellow," which feels believable (Bellow was, after all, born in Montreal), as does his claim that he wrote his first novel on a Remington 22 that once belonged to Chester Himes, but then he brings up his "old friend Walt Whitman." The fact is, he's entered into a camaraderie with every author he's ever loved—and he sees no reason why everyone else can't be in their gang as well.

Laferrière's primary concern is the freedom of the imagination. As a result, reading him can have a pharmaceutical effect; his sentences and images unlock neurotransmitters. He considers himself *un écrivain-ami* (a writer-friend). His aim is not to dazzle you with his prowess and wisdom, but rather to make you laugh, to console you, to share tales, to let you know that you aren't alone. A champion of other writers, he constantly reminds you that great books are treasure chests waiting to be opened. He's able to make you prefer a bottle of bad wine to a bottle of good wine, because, as he argues, that's the power of literature.

He's also been called *un homme-livre*: a man-book. In his world, anything can be part of a story. "As soon as a person passes in front of me," he confides, "they become a fictional character." He, too, can come across like a quasi-fictional entity, likely because he also happens to be the protagonist in his novels. He has written of how F. Scott Fitzgerald seemed to him to have decided to become a character in a book. Laferrière seems to have done the same thing.

"I wrote these books to understand what I was doing with my life," he notes. And his books consistently grapple with the fact that he became a writer. In his novels, he often writes about writing about what he's writing about. In person, he glides between tenses, speaking about past events as if they were in the future, or speaking about his childhood in the present tense. He sometimes speaks of himself as a character in the third person: "He wanted to become a writer." When I pointed out this habit to him, Laferrière brought up Norman Mailer's usage of the self-referential third person as it relates to Thucydides's usage of same in *The History of the Peloponnesian War*. "Thousands of years ago, Thucydides was like, 'This is a war that deserves Thucydides.' *Il est fou ce type!*"

His books are as engorged with cultural references as they are self-referential. Laferrière is indebted to Virginia Woolf, not only in his reliance on stream of consciousness, but also for the simple reason that he mentions her repeatedly in his writing. He continually evokes the writers and artists he loves. Other motifs recur and return throughout his output, as in a zoetrope: swaying branches, slowly falling leaves, the nape of a woman's neck. Amplifying these echoes, the same characters keep popping up: a young girl in a yellow dress from his childhood; his grandmother; the Vodoun *lwa* Legba, a demi-god who inhabits the threshold between this world and the other.

His use of repetition, as a literary device, suggests a kinship to Marguerite Duras. Both writers like to repeat certain crucial lines, often with only slight variations. This approach is rare in contemporary English-language writing nowadays, as editors insist on striking repetitions from the manuscript page. But as Duras knew, repetition is a musical technique. In plain terms: it's what songs do. Lyricism isn't the only effect of repetition. As Borges has written, "Destiny loves repetitions." Everything in nature seeks to make copies of itself. Perhaps repetition in literature brings the reader closer to life?

I can envision Laferrière wondering why Poe might have used these lines in the same paragraph: "To and fro in the seven chambers there stalked, in fact, a multitude of dreams. And these—the dreams—writhed in and about, taking hue from the room… And then, for a moment, all is still, and all is silent… And now again, the music swells, and the dreams live, and writhe to and fro more merrily than ever, taking hue from the many-tinted windows." Taking hue to and fro. Poe even ends that story, "The Masque of the Red Death," with four lines that begin with the same word: *And*; *and*; *and;* and *and*. Repeating lines can entice, even hypnotize, if done properly. And, like Poe, and Borges, and Duras, Laferrière has a catchy way of getting in your head, lulling you into his lullaby—then striking with unexpected dissonance, or radical clarity. All of this occurs merely in the periphery of the work; most readers barely register it; in fact, the idea is likely for it to be essentially unnoticed. Anyway, it can no more be seized and held up to the light as the intangible figure of the Red Death itself.

Laferrière says that the key to all of his subsequent works can be found in his first novel, *How to Make*

Love to a Negro Without Getting Tired. It opens with two twenty-something friends who don't appear to be doing much in a rat-hole of an apartment in the Quartier Latin. "Listen to this, man," says one of them, trying to convince the other that Freud invented jazz, as proven by his readings of page 68 and 69 of *Totem and Taboo* in the metre of Quranic verse over Charlie Parker records.[2] They listen to "Ko-Ko" (1945), a breakneck bebop masterpiece renowned both for its harmonic ambiguity and the way it lifts riffs from other tracks. "Ko-Ko" has been described as "a ping-pong ball being blown by a fan in a very small room"—not unlike the whirl of allusions in that opening scene of Laferrière's first manuscript.

-----

2   Attempts to uncover the specific passages referred to on pages 68 and 69 of *Totem and Taboo: Resemblances Between the Mental Lives of Savages and Neurotics* lead to the realization that those page numbers vary by edition, as well as by translation. There's a good chance that the material highlighted so specifically, yet so utterly uncertainly, derives from the long essay that makes up *Totem and Taboo*'s second chapter, which analyzes purification rites between the living and the dead, notably the washing of bodies in water. Pattern-seekers might also connect this act of misdirection to one of the three verses from the Quran quoted in *How to Make Love*'s opening chapter: "You merge night into day and day into night; You bring the living out of the dead and the dead out of the living." Additionally, none of the numbers of the *surahs* excerpted by our unreliable narrator in that opening chapter actually correspond to those he's referring to in the Quran.

There isn't much action, but something's going on. The apartment reeks of sweet resin incense the friends are burning. They drink tea steeped on an alcohol lamp. Nebulous artworks surround them: Vodoun *vévés*[3]; the effigy of an ancient Egyptian princess called Taiah[4]; a print of Dante Gabriel Rossetti's *Beata Beatrix*. The narrator points out a copy of Swinburne's *Fata Morgana* that they're reading. This could either be the French version of Algernon Charles Swinburne's *Laus Veneris* (1866), published by Éditions Fata Morgana in France[5]; or Henry Swinburne's centuries-old description of a sea-surface mirage seen from the shore[6]; or a reference to how, in

3 Geometrical drawings that represent spirits.

4 It isn't clear who, exactly, this princess might be. The Russian symbolist poet Maximilian Voloshin was known, in early 20th century literary circles, to have a reproduction of a sculpture of Egypt's Queen Mutnedjmet that he called Princess Taiah.

5 Like *How to Make Love*, *Laus Veneris* is an epic hymn to love, sections of which are a lust-letter to Venus: "Her gateways smoke with fume of flowers and fires... Her beds are full of perfume and sad sound."

6 Henry Swinburne's *Travels in the Two Sicilies* (1783) translates the following letter written by Father Ignazio Angelucci, which was included in Athanasius Kircher's *Ars Magna Lucis et Umbrae* (1646):

"On the fifteenth of August, 1643, as I stood at my window, I was surprised with a most wonderful, delectable vision. The sea that washes the Sicilian shore swelled up, and became, for ten miles in length, like a chain of dark mountains; while the waters near our Calabrian

Swinburne's verses, "Everything is suggestive of imagery; but when one attempts to grasp the imagery it proves a *fata morgana*, which disappears."[7] Or it could be something else altogether; or nothing at all. Either way, the effect is the same: whatever we are trying to hang onto melts into mist. Why? That's for the reader to decide. But one thing is certain: within the flurry of highbrow-primitivist references, a new voice was making itself heard, simultaneously atonal and melodic, poetic and humorous, erudite and charming, beating to its own pulpy RaRa rhythm.

As with all poetry, the musicality of his prosody can at times be impervious to translation. His translator, the novelist David Homel, has rendered his books splendidly into English. Still, it's also worth reading Laferrière in French, if possible. Another challenge

---

coast grew quite smooth, and in an instant appeared as one clear polished mirror, reclining against the aforesaid ridge. On this glass was depicted, in *chiaroscuro*, a string of several thousands of pilasters, all equal in altitude, distance, and degree of light and shade. In a moment they lost half their height, and bent into arcades, like Roman aqueducts. A long cornice was next formed on the top, and above it rose castles innumerable, all perfectly alike. These soon split into towers, which were shortly after lost in colonnades, then windows, and at last ended in pines, cypresses, and other trees, even and similar. This is the *Fata Morgana*, which, for twenty-six years, I had thought a mere fable."

7   Richard Henry Stoddard, in his introduction to *The Poems of Algernon Charles Swinburne* (1884).

is that his books overlap and occasionally cannibalize each other—a process exacerbated by his proclivity for rewriting books and then re-issuing them under the same title. "I've redone at least six books," he clarifies. "It terrorizes professors and translators. I made over 1,300 changes to *A Drifting Year* [originally published in French in 1994; the reworked version was released in 2012]. I also added another 150 pages to *Dining With the Dictator* recently."

That multiple versions exist of his books adds layers to his shapeshifting mystique. But beyond antagonizing professors and translators, some of the revisions he's made could also derive from the fact that Laferrière can be—and has been—deserving of criticism. His earliest novels, necessarily products of their time, at times harbour attitudes, whether casual or overt, that are unacceptable today. As Lori Saint-Martin has demonstrated, his clearly antiracist stance is offset by a tendency to espouse sexist stereotypes.[8] Although he revels in the hedonics of discrimination, his narrator seems unaware of the ways in which he, too, is prejudiced. Reading his early works is a reminder that challenging one aspect of the status quo can mean perpetuating other inequalities. Without doing comparative analyses of the different versions he's published of the same books, I suspect that, regardless of what reasons a writer might give for deciding to embark on overhauling earlier works,

---

8   "One Oppression Can Hide Another," *Voix and Images*, December 2011.

it would be hard to resist undoing mistakes, especially those made glaring by posterity. That said, as Laferrière also writes: "Only women have counted for me." The most important recurring characters in his works, after himself, are his beloved grandmother, Da, followed by his mother, Marie. If his favourite writers are men whose names start with B (Borges, Bashō, Baldwin, Bulgakov, and Bukowski), he also writes and speaks adoringly about many female writers, including Woolf, Duras, Edwidge Danticat, Gabrielle Roy, and Patricia Highsmith.

Certain quarters have also taken issue with Laferrière's apparent insouciance about interracial relations. Though his approach to identity politics may at first seem to consist primarily of irony (which can incite anger or outrage), as he has stated, "My position as a writer is to allow the voice of those who are anonymous and oppressed by the economic elite, always hungry for more blood, money, and power, to be heard." His further thoughts on cultural appropriation are examined in these conversations, as are his fascinating insights into money—and spirituality.

Laferrière is not a practising believer of any religion, but he often employs Vodoun deities as literary devices, bringing *lwas* into his writing. "The Greeks used their Greek gods and the Romans used Roman gods," he says. "I don't see why a Haitian wouldn't use their gods, like Legba, Zaka, and Ogou." Legba surfaces regularly in his books, on the threshold of the visible and the invisible. Of Erzulie, multifaceted goddess of love and creation, Laferrière has written of how he admires her audacity, her power, her "furious independence." Erzulie is also the deity of flowers, a trope he frequently invokes when writing about Haiti. The same holds true of fruits, especially mangoes—which he likes to eat onstage in front of a live audience when doing a reading.

I enjoyed the absurd complicity of watching him do so at a talk he gave in Montreal shortly before the interviews that make up this book began. I happened to be there on a first (and, ultimately, last) date, with a painter I liked. As with practically everyone I know, she had never read any of Laferrière's books, but she'd heard of him. Either way, she came along. That evening, he ended up reading poems aloud by some of his favourite Haitian poets, including Clément Magloire-Saint-Aude and Carl Brouard. Unfortunately, even live poetry couldn't fix the lack of chemistry between my date and me. The following morning, she posted this line on Facebook, in French: "If you want to feel butterflies in your stomach, shove caterpillars up your ass." The word she used for shove was *crisse*, a formerly sacrilegious slang variation on the name of Christ. In other words: "Jesus caterpillars up your ass." At least there was some poetry to it. And though neither of us ever felt butterflies together, I did end up with a painting of hers, of an open book, on the wall outside my bedroom. A bit of a cliché, sure, but as Laferrière once wrote, "I am interested only in clichés."

Our interviews were conducted in French over five in-person sessions and several phone calls and emails. Portions of the interviews were previously published in *The Paris Review* (Issue 222, Fall 2017). I also briefly spoke with Maggie Berrouët, his wife of 42 years, about her husband's work. She only agreed to the interview, she said, because of her friendship with my mother, Linda Leith—who is also the publisher and editor of this book. A particularly appropriate collaboration, as I first encountered Laferrière in 2010 when he received the Grand Prize at Blue Metropolis, the literary festival she founded. None of this would have happened, in other words, without my mother, and his wife—and his mother, for that matter.

My initial pre-interview with Laferrière took place in Vermont in July of 2014, on the lawn of Middlebury College's French department, where he was then writer in residence. He started by cautioning that he is notorious for speaking at length: "I'm not a reticent Evan S. Connell figure—*je me raconte*." He is undeniably voluble—*un bon causeur*—but he can also be aphoristic. "The point of conversations is to leave no trace," as he has written. Fortunately, the subsequent conversations were recorded for posterity.

Our taped interviews began the following month at a tavern next to carré Saint-Louis in Montreal, where several of his books are set. It was there that I first noticed the way he speaks with his hands, with tactility, as if touching the sounds of the words with his fingertips might conjure them into being. I later noticed a passage in one of his books where one of his characters expresses himself "with his long, supple, fragile hands. As he speaks they sketch arabesques as strange and astonishingly complex as ideograms... When you look closer and listen to his words, you see the organic link between the idea and the dance of his hands." I laughed out loud several times that day; I also found myself close to tears. At other times, I wasn't quite sure how to feel, as when he started talking, unprompted, about how nobody goes to writers' funerals, recounting examples of unattended-but-for-him burials.

"But why are you talking about writers' funerals?" I asked.

"Because I am immortal!" he retorted. "I can speak calmly on the subject."

The second interview happened in a nondescript strip-mall near his home. As I walked into Les Galeries Normandie, I imagined him finding poetry in the very ordinariness of the setting. Beyond the blandness of its dull walls and beige tiles, I half expected to come across something universal and timeless in the IGA Extra, or maybe the Nautilus Plus. "There are no places that don't deserve to be literary," as he says. We ended up doing the interview in the back room of the mall's bookstore, Librairie Monet. But first, we had coffee in the food court café. As we walked away, the waitress ran after us with Laferrière's hoodie, which he'd left behind on the back of his chair. Does he often forget things? "No," he replied. "Although I sometimes forget my entire wardrobe in a hotel room when I'm traveling."

"Your entire wardrobe?"

"Yes, all my clothes, shirts, pants, suits. I get home and realize that my suitcase is empty. Or I get a note from the publisher abroad saying that the hotel has contacted them and wants to know what to do with the clothes. That's happened around four or five times."

The next interview took place in Laferrière's home, a calm bungalow with potted hibiscus flowers at the front door. He lives there with Berrouët and their three daughters. A Basquiat print hung on the dining room wall next to Haitian naïve paintings. His small office was cluttered with books by writers whose names begin with the letter B. There was no place at the desk for actual writing, as befits someone who prefers to work in the bathtub. We did the interview at the family dining table. He sat at the head of the table, wielding a fly swatter like a conductor's baton as he spoke.

The year after that interview, we had a dreamlike run-in very early one morning in May. It was shortly before 5 a.m., that predawn witching hour when the last tendrils of night wither into light. Legba's time. I stood in front of my apartment, waiting for my ride to work on a film set, when Dany Laferrière walked by across the street. I called out to say hello. He looked over, deep in thought, a faint patch of cloud around his hair. We met in the middle of the road. No cars passed; it was too early. He wore his usual white button-up shirt. Fallen blossoms decorated the ground. We live twenty minutes apart, by car, on the highway—a two-hour walk—and here he'd wandered, on foot, in the darkness. Had he been up all night? We didn't talk long. He was elsewhere, in a distant land. It felt as though I'd startled him while asleep, or at work, wandering toward the shadowy Shirakawa Barrier on the way to the Interior.

Our final meeting took place in Paris, where he was dwelling in a renovated former monastery in the *10ème*. A fitting locale, as he sees the role of the writer today to be akin to what the role of priests used to be: you marry couples, you hear confessions, you help people imagine something greater. Our conversation took us down Agnès Varda avenues, though a leafy Mavis Gallant park, along the boulevards of Patrick Modiano's *Paris Nocturne*. Everything was out of a story. We came to the stone facade of the Gare du Nord, or, as he called it, "the gateway to the Northern Realms." Over dinner that evening, we shared an order of *cervelle*—that is, we shared a brain, an experience that will be familiar to many of his readers.

—Adam Leith Gollner
Montreal, May 2020

1. HAPPINESS AWAITS

ALG: The image of a mango falling from a tree is found in many of your books.

DL: Yes, the muted sound of the falling mango. When I was a child, when my cousins and I were in bed at night, we listened for that sound so that we'd be able to pinpoint where a mango had fallen. In the morning, when my grandmother Da opened the door and told us to get up, we'd run outside to find the mangoes. A dozen or so would fall every night, and we were three kids, so we had to run to the right spot and get it fast—like a hunt for treasure, or Easter eggs. We'd memorize the places where we'd heard them fall in the night: next to the well, near the park, close to the fence, near the sea. We jumped, we ran, we each tried to pick up as many mangoes possible.

Do you think that played a role in sharpening your memories as a writer?

It was a memory exercise that was linked to something poetic. I like to remember doing that. It's poetic to know that your memory can recall the location of pleasure, where pleasure hides. To find a mango hiding in a grove, or under a leaf. The Japanese poets wrote a lot about that in their haikus. "The mango beneath the leaf."

Who are the Japanese poets who wrote about that idea?

Maybe not about mangoes, more about melons. Bashō did it, Issa did it. "The melon that has rolled out from the leaves." They are always discovering something, a happiness that awaits. I know that pleasure, spotting a mango with its waxy stem. That wax means the mango wasn't picked; it fell from the branch. It was ready. The tree grew, it made a mango, and the mango fell. We waited for the process to be complete. It's not a green mango that's picked unready and then shipped overseas. It's a ripe mango eaten with the sound of its fall. One eats it with the impression of belonging to the universe where the mango tree is, of being an extension of the mango tree. Picking fruit from a mango tree is like tearing children away from their mother. But when the mango falls, it's an offering. A gift. It would be a shame if no one ate it. It would certainly make the mango tree sad. You aren't doing anything wrong by eating it. Quite the opposite; you are participating in the movement of things.

You once wrote that "Nothing is more alive than a red bicycle leaning against a wall." It makes me think of this part of town, of carré Saint-Louis, of old bicycles locked up against fences overgrown with foliage in the summer. For you, does it make you think of Haiti? Or could it be any place at all?

It's a metaphor and it's something real. When I was a kid, I didn't have a bike. But I had a desire for one, and a desire to discover life. I didn't have a bike, but I had the desire for a bike, and isn't that to be more alive than someone who has a bike? I thought so. I had a friend who lived down the street in Petit-Goâve who had a bike, a little red bike with big wheels. I loved it. Simon was his family name. He must have been twelve or thirteen, but he was an imbecile; he didn't even understand generosity. I did everything for him, with him, his homework, you name it. And in the end, he lent me his bike for five minutes when I thought he was going to lend it to me for a whole day. I had to remedy the situation. My desire, my need, had been put in the service of Simon, that pest. I told myself: never again. I decided that I would prefer the taste of desiring the bicycle to that of actually having Simon's bicycle. I became a person who would prefer any red bicycle leaning against a wall more than riding Simon's bicycle.

There's a real outdoor life in Haiti. So many stores are on the sidewalk, or up against walls. The first time I arrived in Port-au-Prince, I couldn't believe all the goods for sale everywhere you walk: clothing boutiques, appliance shops, makeshift restaurants. Everything is on the street.

Yes, and there are so many people out too. You even wonder whether the vendors will sell all their food. There are moments to buy, in the evening, when the prices start to drop. The food there is so perishable.

The question of food in Haiti is an interesting one.

There are more ways to feed yourself there than we might think. It's a complex society that can't be casually judged. We'd be wrong to do that. Our preconceived ideas aren't always right. Things are linked not to how much you earn, but to what the earth has to offer and the price of fruit. A big avocado doesn't cost much, a few mangoes don't cost much, and they suffice for a meal. When I'm in Haiti, I eat avocados and mangoes, and it feels good to eat fallen fruit. I love mangoes and avocados. Enormous ones, with magnificent flavour, at an affordable price. It's strange, it can be hard for people to feed themselves, and yet you find magnificent fruits in nature: mangoes, avocados, guavas, oranges.

The media often focuses on food shortages there; what would you say is really happening in Haiti today?

It depends. There are zones in Haiti that are harder than others, more desertified. There are some places of real misery. But the question of food itself is quite complex, because it's sunny and hot, and fruit and vegetables grow everywhere. There are many markets, little produce stalls, selling yams, vegetables, fruits, pineapples, oranges. Documentaries about Haiti tell you that there isn't a single tree there, that the country is a pebble. It's not true. It's a green country.

There are also coffee trees everywhere—and coffee is another one of your favourite subjects.

Coffee is from that same time for me, a time of discovery. A mango you encounter whole, but I first became acquainted with coffee in a diluted sense. Because it is a kind of initiation. You don't start your life drinking coffee. You need to wait until around the age of nine before they'll give you grown-up strength coffee. And coffee in Haiti is strong coffee.

Nine years old is still pretty young to be drinking strong espresso.

That's true, but when it's a profession that involves members of your own family, it's not surprising. My grandfather was a coffee buyer and speculator who supplied Italian coffee producers. I've written about this in *An Aroma of Coffee*. Coffee is my culture. I always saw my grandfather buying beans and my grandmother drinking coffee. When coffee is your culture, you do start young. If your family produces alcohol, you learn to drink early. If you grow up with a baker, you become skilled in making bread early on. Whenever your home is impregnated with something, you become a specialist years before others would. For us, it was coffee. In little espresso cups though, not the mugs North Americans use.

Tell me about Haitian coffee culture.

Drinking coffee there is an *art de vivre*. It's not merely a drug; it's an art. My grandmother didn't drink coffee to stay awake. She did it because it's an exceptional beverage and she could offer some to people passing by in the street. The offering was part of our culture. Same as with a ripe mango: the mango tree offers its mango to the child, and my grandmother offered her coffee to passersby. It's the reaching out of the arm, a branch being a tree's arm. Everything is at the end of the arm.

In *An Aroma of Coffee* you talk of the way that coffee can erase the borders between young and old. How so?

Coffee is a universe: it occupies space. You can sense the movement of coffee in the house. It wakes everyone up with its marvelous aroma. I spent my childhood at my grandmother's feet, and she was always drinking and commenting on her coffee. Whenever she finished a cup, she asked me to fetch her some water, which she used to drink up the dregs of coffee powder at the bottom of the cup. Coffee creates habits, and it helps the child who is a young writer to characterize other members of the household. If there's someone in the family who doesn't drink coffee, it's as though you are in a religious household and one family member doesn't believe in God. It's accepted, but it's a scandal. So, I come from a family of coffee drinkers. Lots of relatives used to stop by for coffee for just long enough to exchange a bit of information: how is the little one, is *madame* sick, how is life, *quoi*. You soon get a sense of the people who come for coffee and who they are. My childhood revolves around coffee.

You were as precocious a coffee drinker as you were a reader.

I don't even remember when I started reading—it's so far back. I have the impression that I started reading without knowing how to read. Kids do that sometimes. They recognize groupings of words from the times others read to them, and they start making links with images, and are soon repeating phrases. That's how I learned to read. I read all the books in the house, from children's books to fairy tales to Cinderella stories to any book at all. My aunt Renée was the librarian at the small library in Petit-Goâve, and I'd bring her food and we'd chat. I'd read books about science. I was young, so I didn't understand anything—but I read. The mayor's son lived in France, where he was a doctor, and he sent over some books to start the library. It was mainly a medical library, but it included some very theoretical works on literature and literary schools. Maurice Blanchot. Really intellectual books, but I read them anyway, as though they too were fables. I read the words, I looked at them, I didn't feel obliged to understand.

Reading Blanchot was so helpful to me when I was working on my first book. Especially the way he describes writing as an impossible act, like the experience of being lost, of accomplishing something that cannot be accomplished. *The Book to Come* is like a wilderness survival guide for writers. What do you

remember about finding his book in that library when you were a child?

I remember the flavour of the moment, the scent of the food I'd brought for Aunt Renée. I remember our conversations. And the stunning fact that there was almost never anyone else in the library. Aunt Renée didn't mind that. This was her work. She came, and she sat, and when it was time to go home, she locked up and went home. It didn't bother her whether two people had come or none at all. She never complained that people didn't come. I remember leaving the library and walking home. I remember a study book about poetry. I couldn't understand why somebody would write a book to explain a poem. I still don't get why you would want to explain a poem. The pleasure in poetry is shamanic. The sounds we pronounce put us in a state. It's not a question of knowing. I didn't understand, and I was impressed because I didn't understand.

There's something important about the idea of not understanding in much of your work.

Yes, absolutely.

The senses seem to be what really matter.

Vision.

And sensuality.

The senses are the essence.

"The eye, the ear, the mind in action." Tell me a bit about that. Even when you speak about that library, your memories are linked to your senses.

When I speak of a book, I remember the moment I read it and the odours that surrounded me as I was reading. I remember that before I remember the content of the book. And I remember the well-being I felt while I was reading. My rapport with the world is very physical. The intellectual world for me is very physical. For me the world is never completely, solely intellectual. It has to have an impact on the body, on the senses. I come from a Caribbean natural world that is intoxicating, if one can put it this way. I grew up in a milieu where fruits rotted on the trees. Vendors couldn't sell all their fruits. So I always smelled those scents. It's a country on the equator. Night falls quickly. Cities can be identified by their odours. When I was a child, Port-au-Prince smelled like jasmine in the evening. Or ylang-ylang. People could be identified by their odours. Country folk smell like leaves, the scent of a tree. A *paysan* is a tree that walks. We call them *nègres-feuille* [leaf Negroes] because they always smell like tree leaves. They do everything with leaves. I remember covering cauldrons with large banana leaves. And making something with corn—I don't remember.

I loved eating ground cornmeal polenta cooked with leaves in Haiti: *maïs moulu avec feuille.*

There are so many different kinds of leaves. I never understood the idea that Haiti is a leafless desert. We are close to leaves, to odours, to colours also.

Tropical flowers and butterflies abound. And people's homes there are painted in such bright colours, as are shop signs and *tap-tap* buses. The same with all the artworks you see for sale in the streets. Those vibrant hues form an elemental part of your lexicon: red bicycles, turquoise waves, yellow dresses, purple kisses. You've even written of wanting to lose awareness of your being in order "to blend into nature and become a leaf."

Because I wanted to be as true as possible to my sensibility, I wrote with this idea of the senses—the presence of the senses. That's how I navigate the world, the universe I'm in. I associate the senses with being intoxicated by aromas. It's animalistic. Imagine someone like me arriving in Montreal and being completely lost without those odours and those colours. When winter arrives, we're lost. People are all bundled up. In Haiti, it's always the same season, the same palette of colours, the same light—in December you maybe need to put a shirt on. But in Montreal, the first thing

I learned is that colours are seasonal. Seasons are what direct us. Nature steers things. There are also different smells for different seasons, for snow smothers all scents. And there's a type of food for when it's cold as well. I didn't know that people could live seasonally. So I had no frame of reference here. My senses weren't being nourished by familiar scents and colours. I had to reinvent myself, to find new ways of orienting myself, using new scents and new colours.

What effect did that have on your writing?

The idea of the senses is what permitted me, as a writer, to not aim to produce a logical kind of literature based on rationality and intelligence, but rather to produce something that aimed to *seduce*, not to convince. The aim was for the reader to be encircled by these perfumes I'm trying to describe—in activating senses that aren't logical—so that he or she drops the need to judge. They enter the universe the way you enter a painting. The universe invades them, the way a primitive painting can overcome the viewer. They are in the universe. This is why I often use short phrases and images in my writing: to reduce as much as possible the distance between the reader and the odours and colours evoked by the book. Readers shouldn't feel the distance; there should be no interference. They barely have time to read a pretty sentence and to smell it before they're hit with another scent entirely. Pretty soon, they're intoxicated. They can no longer analyze it or look at it critically, they're simply caught in the profusion of colours and perfumes. I mean, it isn't that organized. That's the way I am, so that's what comes out. When I try to articulate it, it sounds like a scam.

I love that moment in _The Lover_ where Duras describes their lovemaking apartment, with all the smells of the street wafting in through the window: "Whiffs of burnt sugar drift into the room, the smell of roasted peanuts, Chinese soups, roast meat, herbs, jasmine, dust, incense, charcoal fires, they carry fire about in baskets here, it's sold in the street." There's something incantatory about overloading the reader with so much sensual detail. It's irresistible. It also reminds me of that passage in _How to Make Love_ where you speak about the smell of poverty, how it's hard to get it out of your clothes. The protagonist decides to hang out in front of an Italian fast-food chain restaurant called Da Giovanni to take on the smell of spaghetti instead.

Yes, it's very physical. It's true that we are the odour that we emit. We become the odour that impregnates us. And we become the odour of what we are. A Haitian poet I admire says that death smells like orange blossoms. I hope that the final scent I'll have in my nostrils, before dying, will be that of mangoes. The aroma of a good Francis mango, Haiti's national mango. When I go to Port-au-Prince, one of the first things I do is stock up on mangoes. I always have mangoes in my room. When you open the door, you smell the scent of mangoes. I keep them there, and I let them ripen completely and their perfume suffuses the room. It's my favourite smell. On my deathbed, they should put a bowl of very ripe mangoes next to me, to fill the room with the smell of my childhood.

2. BUILDING A CATHEDRAL

In one of your books, you mention that Kurt Vonnegut, Jr., called you "the fastest titler in America." What is the importance of a title to you?

A title is important to me, but it isn't important for all writers. The greatest writers are the only ones allowed to use bad titles. A medium-grade or slightly good writer should above all strive to attract attention to their book with a striking title. Once you have the right title, you've completed most of the work of writing a book.

Ha! There's often something provocative in your titles.

A title gives a book its ambiance. One could say that a title like *The Almost Forgotten Art of Doing Nothing* is an effective title. The same with *Cette grenade dans la main du jeune nègre est-elle une arme ou un fruit?* (Translated as *Why Must a Black Writer Write About Sex?*, the title's verbatim meaning would be *Is That Grenade/ Pomegranate in the Young Negro's Hand a Weapon or a Fruit?*) But that isn't all I was trying to do. I also published books entitled *An Aroma of Coffee* and *Heading South*. It isn't always a special title, like *Le goût des jeunes filles*. [Translated as *Dining With the Dictator*, its actual meaning is *The Taste of Young Girls*.] A good title should warm the reader's heart in a bookstore, creating an immediate empathy with the book and making it unnecessary for the writer to explain themselves too much.

What do you mean?

Only a truly great writer can call their book something like *Man's Hope*, as Malraux did. You have to be an immense writer to get away with calling your book *Man's Hope*. A lesser writer would have to spend countless expository pages explaining why they called their book *Man's Hope*—which Malraux doesn't have to do, because he's Malraux. Great writers don't need to explain their titles. If you aren't a great writer, you have to find another way of not having to explain your titles. In creating an immediate rapport with the reader through the title, you bypass the need to explain it. If you are charming, you don't need to explain yourself. And that's the thing with a title like *How to Make Love to a Negro Without Getting Tired*. There's no need to explain it.

Without asking you to explain it, what was your motivation behind that particular title?

It was to escape from the kind of French literature where titles were quite staid, self-serious, over-important—titles like *À la recherche du temps perdu*. Titles that let you know they are literary, intellectual, thinking-person books. I wondered if you couldn't do a smart, literary book while also having a fun title, like *Everything You Always Wanted to Know About Sex But Were Afraid to Ask*. I tried to put myself into that category, rather than being someone who thinks they need to have an important title. The gods struck me with that very first title.

Humour plays a part in the title. Is there an element of anger or mockery to it, as well?

No, no that's not it. It was more about having a rapport with literature, but in a casual, unconventional way. It was more about what sort of writer I wanted to be: laid back.

Did your book *I Am A Japanese Writer* really start with the title?

It certainly did. My publisher in Paris was interested by the way Caribbean and Creole writers treat the question of identity. I wasn't at all interested in that. I wanted to approach the subject not at all from a perspective tied to colonialism or politics or the left or the right. I wanted to tackle it rather in a strictly linguistic sense.

The book essentially imagines what the outcome would be if you actually wrote a book called *I am A Japanese Writer*. To be clear: the plot is about you— or your narrative stand-in—contemplating writing a book by that title. But it never actually gets written.

That's right. Except in reality I actually did write a book called *I am a Japanese Writer*.

You often write about being between worlds, about dissolving thresholds or frontiers. Things are not exactly clear in your works; they are in between dream and reality, between memory and imagination, even between art and life.

A writer is someone who crosses frontiers without being stopped, and without getting caught, both in the imaginary sense and in reality. To read is to be able to change centuries. That's the power of literature. It erases borders. They say you can't be a Japanese writer if you don't know Japan. So I chose a country that I didn't know that is far away and I said, there: I am a Japanese writer.

Much of the book explores the reactions that such an arrestingly-titled book would engender. In the early chapters, you anxiously wonder if you are even allowed to call yourself a Japanese writer. The country's legal system weighs in, hoping to prevent your book from being published. A counter-attack is published in Japan entitled *I am A Malagasy Writer*.

The people of Japan become outraged at the idea of a black writer writing a book about Japanese identity.

At one point, you write, "I don't even care about identity... I'm writing this book precisely to escape that whole thing."

Yes. Who can stop me from being a Japanese writer? Nobody. And now it's actually coming out in a Japanese translation!

How do you see the idea of cultural appropriation?

I don't know what people are talking about. Nothing that I write comes from myself alone. The alphabet and grammar existed before I did. The cannon of global literature that is a concentration of the planet itself helps me think, write, and even live. I forget what country those I'm indebted to come from. Culture is a link that unites people. *I Am a Japanese Writer* is dedicated to anyone who ever wanted to be someone else. But I am also not against the trials, when someone feels that they've been wronged in some manner and they need to pursue justice. The cultural milieu does not consist exclusively of culture, just as a concert doesn't consist exclusively of music. You need people from a wide variety of trades to stage a concert, and they have no obligation to like music at all, let alone the music of the artists in that particular show. I hear foolishness on both sides. It's important to remember that the cultural sphere is not exempt from all the corruption that exists in other spheres. There are some people who, if they were allowed, would only hire people from their own families. Maybe that's what people are talking about when they talk about cultural appropriation.

Cultural appropriation is a form of nepotism?

It's the idea of "keeping it in the family"—in the same class, race, sex, and so on. These people seem to be suffocating, to be unable to find a breathable place to realize their dreams. For a dream to come true in art, you often need enormous machinery and support systems, all of which require strong networks. And that's not what people are talking about, unfortunately, on either side of the divide. It's become an ideological subject, rather than a practical, technical one.

Do you think it depends on the background of the person who is doing the appropriating?

It's a question of class but disguised by pseudo-intellectual reflections. A minority, through its networks, confiscates all the cake. And to defend itself, the majority ends up acting in bad faith. It lashes out at culture itself. It takes back what it had shared with the whole world in the hope of coming to an understanding of the human condition. You'll note that I'm using the words *minority* and *majority*, and we tend to always place the minority in the role of the victim. We refuse, on racial grounds, to add all the victims together into unified whole, which constitutes the majority. It isn't a question of white, black, yellow, red—it's a question of those in power seizing everything and telling you it all belongs to them, and of those who do not have a voice. If we view things that way, it all becomes clearer. Everything got all mixed up when race became confused with culture.

You decided to speak out on Canadian news television about a photograph that surfaced in 2019 of

Justin Trudeau at a costume party many years earlier. When he made a public apology, he explained that the photo was taken at an Arabian Nights theme party where he went as Aladdin, with dark makeup covering his face. What was it that stood out to you about that image?

At the time that photo was released, I was in Montreal and I felt that a critical error was made in reading the situation. Aladdin is not a human being, but a literary character—and I had the sense that 90 percent of people had forgotten that important detail.

The point you made, if I can summarize, is that Trudeau wasn't actually in blackface, as certain quarters had been suggesting, or even in brownface—he was dressed up as Aladdin.

I'm a writer, so I couldn't let that aesthetic mistake slip by. My intervention wasn't a political act but rather an aesthetic one. I said it and then I moved on.

The effect your intervention had on me was to make me go read *Aladdin; Or The Wonderful Lamp*, the original version—where the very first line states that Aladdin is actually Chinese, not Middle Eastern. It seemed fitting. And it reminded me of how you once mentioned, in an email, that you like the idea of inhabiting a language. "A language is a territory," as you put it. Please tell me a bit more about this.

I should have said that a language is more than a territory. Or that it is a limitless territory. It's any place where those who speak that language are. A language carries within itself many diverse phenomena. A language embraces you. Its erotic characteristics permit intimate connections. A language makes babies who go elsewhere and who end up rubbing against all sorts of other languages. We see it when we're working on the dictionary at the *Académie*: words are not always born from one single territory. The goal of a language is to travel, to cross the world, in every sense, and to learn every other language.

In 2013, you were elected to the *Académie Française*, the first-ever Haitian or Québécois writer to join their ranks.

They had to first sort out whether I was even admissible. You're supposed to be *French*. It turns out it wasn't a written rule. At the time the rules were written, they couldn't even imagine including someone not born in France, or a French colony or *département*, or a naturalized Frenchman. A Haitian in Montreal is none of the above. To be eligible, you also have to live in France—which I did not. So the question became: is it the *Académie Française* as in *the French language*? Or as in *France*? The President of the Republic decided the question: it's the Academy of the French language. This decision made it possible for my candidacy to go forward. Elections were held; they inducted me.

How does that work?

It can take several rounds of voting as a successful investiture requires an absolute majority, meaning at least 21 votes out of 40. There can be several candidates for a *fauteuil*, and the candidate who gets into the *Académie* is not the person who gets the most votes, but the person who gets the absolute majority. It's quite rare that a candidate gets an absolute majority on the first round of voting. There can be up to four or five rounds of voting. But if, in the fourth round, nobody gets an absolute majority it's an *élection blanche*. If you get in on the first round, it's called *une belle éléction*, a home run. I was received with enthusiasm, in the first round of voting. It took Victor Hugo five rounds, Voltaire three!

They bestowed a word on you: *valiant.*

When you join the *Académie*, they give you a word from the French language. They offer it to you. It's a ritual, a tradition. My word was *vaillant*.

Is the idea for you to re-define the word, to elaborate on the definition in some way? What exactly do you do with the word?

It's simply a word that is bestowed on you before you enter the hall for the first time, a word chosen for you by your fellow *Académiciens*. They attributed that particular word to me because they felt it corresponded to my temperament. That I'm a fighter, a *résistant*, someone brave, I suppose.

Is that actually your temperament?

I'm not a risk-seeker, but yes, I'm reasonably persevering. I am a *résistant*. But at the same time, I'm not someone who beats himself to the finish to arrive at something—as you know from my books. But the word they give you, it becomes your word. It remains a part of your induction into the *Académie*. It's the word they attributed to you. The word has to begin with the letter they're working on at that moment. They happened to have arrived at the letter V. So they didn't seek out my word in the absolute; they did so in the V-words. It can land nicely, or badly, depending. It has to be a word they haven't offered before.

What do you actually do there, beneath the dome?

I am part of several commissions, involving the dictionary, literature, and *francophonie*. I attend the weekly *grandes séances* on Thursdays. We do everything from discussing issues relating to the *Académie* and the granting of literary awards and prizes, to revising definitions of words.

How do you discuss a word?

If a word that was used by Flaubert or Césaire and falls into desuetude, if it becomes passé, we still keep it in the dictionary because it was used by an important writer. The dictionary strives to recognize the creativity employed by writers in their use of a term. Our commission not long ago tackled the word *sex*. So we looked at how writers use a word like *sex*—all the different notions, phrases, and implications that have come up over the years. The Marquis de Sade doesn't have the same thoughts on the matter as, say, the Marquise de Sévigné. An ordinary word can take up half a page in the dictionary; a word like *sex* can run at six or seven pages.

How did *you* contribute to defining that particular word?

The dictionary doesn't have individual contributions. It's like building a cathedral. The workers are unknown. But one of the things I tend to do is suggest that it might be interesting to have examples of things that aren't from France. If it's a wind, which is a word we worked on recently, does it always have to be the *mistral*? What about the winds of elsewhere? How about zephyrs or siroccos? In French, there exists an enormous variety of classifications, proverbs, and witticisms about winds. There are winds that push ships as well as winds that come from the gut: the noisy, bodily winds of Rabelais. *All* shadings have to be in the dictionary. And in circumstances like this, you realize that people always remain, in a way, children—even august adults. Words that concern the inner workings of the human body can still provoke a smile, or a laugh, even within the *Académie Française*.

So it's normal for me to be laughing right now?

Yes. It is appropriate for a person to laugh in imagining that scenario.

Okay, but I still don't think you've answered my question on your contribution to the definition of the word *sex*. You discussed it, but what did you discuss?

It would be inappropriate for an *Académicien* to suggest any personal contribution to a definition.

Did you bring up any specific aspects that were different from what others were saying, or did you suggest considerations that weren't already in the dictionary?

I certainly did, but the whole idea is for the cathedral builders to remain anonymous.

You have written that for you everything is serious and nothing is.

Everything is serious because I honestly don't have a lot of time. Nothing is serious in the sense that I spend that time not obeying rules and orthodoxy. A child plays with gravity—but they know it's a game.

You say that you "hate authenticity" and "real" life. Why is that?

Because it all already exists. The word *real* is always abusive. The abuse is that something else is always implied by it. Everything is real, so as soon as someone says the word *real* and wants to tell you *real* things, they are simply going to tell you things that they're interested in and that are invariably negative for you. Whenever someone says, "I'm going to tell you something real," it ends up being something aggressive.

But can't someone talk about reality in a positive way?

It's always *their* reality they're imposing on you. It's not reality, it's not real. They're simply placing their truth and their reality over reality. Reality exists: there's no need to get worked up over it. We're surrounded with it. We can't even escape it. There's no point even glossing over it or making interminable discourses over it. We are in it. So as soon as someone brings up something *real*, it's automatically not reality but rather a construction. It's their perception, their ideology, their principles. And that is rarely something good for you, and it's usually something against you.

So it's inevitably a confrontation between versions of reality?

Yes. Because when there's nothing wrong, no one cares. It's only when there's a problem that someone starts defining or redefining reality.

You are about to start working on a new book of poetry, your first book of verse. Do you already have some ideas or inspiration that you wish to explore in these poems?

I can't say much about the book, especially as it's a book of poetry. For me, poetry is not thought, it just alights. I am waiting impatiently for that. I have the impression it will take place in the nighttime with hoods from Port-au-Prince who don't expect much from life. That might be the origin of the title: *Vite, je n'ai pas que ça à faire.* (*Quick, I Have Other Things to Do Besides This.*) At this very moment, on April 1, 2020, I am preparing to write it, my first book of poems. My friend Alain Mabanckou asked me to put together a poetry collection for his new series being published by Éditions du Seuil, in Paris. I'm not too sure what the book will become. I'm raring to get inside of it. *Vite, je n'ai pas que ça à faire.*

Do you see the process of writing poems as being similar to writing fiction? How does it differ?

I don't write enough poetry to really know the difference between poems and prose. In fact, I only write poetry.

Yet your 2009 book *The Return* alternates between prose and verse. You've used this approach in other books, too, such as *Eroshima* and *A Drifting Year*. Why?

Because *The Return* is, first and foremost, a poetic book. Whether the sections are in verse or in prose, it is poetic throughout. I initially wrote it all in verse. I wrote it in Port-au-Prince: standing up, walking down the street, in the car, sitting at friends' places. But in transcribing the notebooks, I realized that the text I'd written needed some context and some explanation, and so the prose sections are more to provide context. The prose is the jewel-box, and the verse is the jewel.

Did you want the mix of forms to be apparent to readers? There's no explanation given in the book. And I must confess: I didn't even realize that some parts were written in verse when I first read it.

Good. I wanted people to not notice that it is made up of poems. I wanted them just to read it as they would a novel. And I like changing a lot. I like to vary things. I didn't want it to be only in one poetic form. Also, if it was in only one form, I'd have fewer readers. No, really. I would have had maybe 500 readers—under 1,000 for sure. But as is, it had 100,000 readers. Readers see it as a novel, not a book of poetry. It's a *roman poétique*.

Have you ever cared about the size of your readership?

Yes and no. I always wanted readers. You don't even need a lot of readers, just *some* readers. Just enough readers to win my freedom. When you have too many readers you have to answer to another boss: the reader. As soon as you sell below a certain preordained number of books, you're in trouble. Whereas someone who sells far fewer books will never be bothered by that whole side of publishing, because they have a healthy balance between their symbolic weight and the size of their readership.

The Return **was a hit, and it remains one of your key works. Do you know of any other writers who've written books that combine verse with prose? Your beloved Bashō does it—albeit not in the exact manner you do. And Virginia Woolf spoke of *The Waves* as "a play-poem." But it differs in obvious ways. Anyone else?**

There must be some other writers who've done it, but I don't know who they are. I don't know of anyone else who uses the approach I do. The idea is for an ordinary reader to read it even though it's a poem.

Gogol envisioned *Dead Souls* as a "poem in prose," or a "novel in verse," but within a traditional storytelling format.

Bukowski, too, wrote narrative poems. *Love Is a Dog from Hell* is *récits* in verse, although there's no prose embedded among the verses themselves, as in my case. But perhaps that book, as well, gives readers the impression they're reading fiction, as opposed to poetry.

***The Return* has an intriguing title. The full title in French, *L'Enigme du retour*, is an allusion to Naipaul's *The Enigma of Arrival*, which is itself a reference to a painting by De Chirico, *The Enigma of the Arrival and the Afternoon*, which was actually named by Apollinaire.**

Yes! For me, there was also a linguistic and philosophical aspect to the title that attracted me. I found that the enigma of arrival is not all that enigmatic. It's in fact quite normal to feel displaced when you arrive somewhere new for the first time, whether it's New York or Bombay. On the other hand, I found that the experience of *returning* somewhere after years in exile, *returning* to the place we came from, and realizing we don't understand the rules of life there—I found *that* enigmatic. After decades away, it is enigmatic to return to our birthplace and no longer understand the things that structured our life during our childhood and adolescence. It is more enigmatic for someone to return home and say, *I don't understand* than it is for someone to arrive in New York City and say, *I don't understand.*

That's true.

The word enigma doesn't only connote a misunderstanding or misinterpretation, but also an inexplicability that questions itself. Something enigmatic is something that *should* be understood, but that includes a silence at the heart of the interrogation. It isn't just a questioning. It isn't just, *I don't understand New York, how does New York work?* It's also, *Why do I not understand? I should be able to understand.* What's enigmatic in the return is when a person loses their sense of self to the point of not understanding the rules and the rituals of their own homeland.

Naipaul's book is also a precursor to yours, a Caribbean expat's description of life in his adopted home, in his case, in rural England.

What really interested me was Naipaul's insolence. A Caribbean writer arrives in England and starts to discuss the country with the same hauteur as a Brit going on about a little tropical island. I found it formidable. He finds the seeming orderliness of provincial England to be quite beneath him. I don't remember the book as much as I remember its effect on me—the realization that it was possible to speak from that position.

It's also a book about writing, like so many of your own books.

That is a constant with Naipaul, that continual reflection on literature and on the act of writing. He writes as though stunned that he is a writer. In his astonishment, he keeps analyzing that occurrence, turning it over, looking at it from all angles. It's as though it couldn't possibly be—and yet it happened.

3. THE GREAT SORCERER'S SPELL

We're currently in a part of town that figures prominently in your life and in your books, on rue Saint-Denis at carré Saint-Louis, at the sort of tavern you lovingly describe in *The Return* as a "crummy bar where you could spend all day over a warm beer." Why here?

This is first of all the Latin Quarter, the heart of Montreal's Quartier Latin, right next to carré Saint-Louis. We're three houses over from the apartment I lived in when I wrote my first novel, which describes this very place. This is where I invented myself. This was the precise site of rupture. This is where I had to define who I was. Was I an exile? An exile is someone who remembers themselves, but who cannot return to the place where much of their life happened, where their sensibilities were formed, where people they know still live, people they love or hate. I wanted to be a traveller, so I needed to invent a new universe. And the first thing I did was to write a novel in which the word Haiti doesn't appear once. My first book.

At one point in that book, *How to Make Love to a Negro Without Getting Tired*, someone asks the main character, your authorial stand-in, where he's from, and he responds that he is from Madagascar—on Thursday nights.

Yes, he's covering his tracks. He says he's from Harlem, or the Ivory Coast, or Madagascar on Thursday nights. For me, that moment of rupture was something I wanted to enact voluntarily. To be from Haiti, to be imbued with coffee, the scent of mangoes, the taste of avocados, the smell of leaves, of jasmine, of ylang-ylang: those things came from my birth. They weren't things I had decided. But I could decide to be in Montreal. And for me, that was it. A writer is able to create a universe. So I created this universe with that book. I severed my ties with Haiti to break the great sorcerer's spell—that of the dictator, who says, *You will be obsessed with me, and you will think only of me. I can do other things, but you, you will think of avenging yourself, of getting worked up, and you will think of nothing but me.*

So, what did you do?

I believed I had to pretend, first of all. The biggest school of all is the school of make-believe. I pretended that I forgot the dictator by writing a book in which neither he, nor the universe to which he belongs—not even my mother—appears. By pretending, I ended up creating a new universe.

In the text of *How to Make Love*, you described the act of writing that book as your only chance. It needed to be, you felt, "the masterpiece that will get you out of your hole."

For me, that's what this space here represents. I can tell you the story of this universe, carré Saint-Louis, rue Saint-Denis, 3670 rue Saint-Denis, across the street from rue Cherrier, and Café Cherrier, the little boutiques on Saint-Denis below Sherbrooke, the park itself, with its small fountain, its wildlife, the people, the vagrants, the neighbourhood's bourgeois residents, the travellers passing through, the young women from the anglo part of town, from McGill, who come to this part of town looking for adventure. All that is in my books, as it is in reality. *How to Make Love to a Negro Without Getting Tired* is a dog pissing, demarcating its territory. It's the only territory I marked off in Montreal. And even when there are events that don't occur here in my other books, I return here. This space here is the space of conquest. Conquest from below. The conquest of the poor— but conquest nonetheless. It's not Balzac's *À nous deux, Paris*. It's just a man, a young man, alone, who believes that the things he names belong to him. Or that he belongs to the things he names. By describing them in my writing, I belong to this space here. At the start, I believed that I was writing my books, that my books were coming from me, but in time I ended up realizing that I myself came from my books. That's it. We see things; they belong to us. We put them in books and find ourselves within those things as a narrator. And then we belong to those things. These two moments are the grand lesson of literature. It's more interesting to belong to things than to have things belong to us. It's more relaxing. When things belong to us, we have to protect the treasure. But when we belong to things, it's up to things to protect us, so we can sleep in peace. *Tout le temps qu'on ne possède pas, on peut dormir en paix.*

Sleeping is a major theme in your writing.

I'm part of a long line of primitive painters who always inhabited that way of doing things. The surrealists tried to tap into that as well. I remember when André Breton went to Haiti and saw paintings by Hector Hippolyte, he commented that Hippolyte easily accomplishes what they were trying to do with surrealism. Which is to say Hippolyte isn't producing a literature that gives the impression of a dream; he's *in* the dream. He is dreaming. To understand the extremely sophisticated poetry of Clément Magloire-Saint-Aude, you have to realize that he is dreaming. "I am the sleeper." He says it often—he's horizontal. Like Davertige, taking the sea in his arms. He has the world in his arms. He's a man-island. A man standing up aims to convince; he makes a speech. The man lying down dreams. He meditates, he looks at the clouds. In my books there is always someone asleep, an immobile character in the midst of reveries.

Bouba is recumbent, on a couch, from the beginning of your very first book. He doesn't care if the world blows itself up—he's sleeping. And he is simultaneously "purifying the universe."

Bouba is the clearest example of it. But Da is a dreamed character as well, a character who is dreaming. She doesn't move; everything moves around her. That's a dreamer, someone in the night who sleeps and who doesn't move whose world is swarming with life. She's immobile. In *Why Must a Black Writ-*

er Write About Sex?, you can't tell if what happened really happened or if it only happened in the bathtub or in the bedroom. The hero of *The Return* speaks of sleep, and we don't know if he really did all the things he describes or if he just stayed in his bathtub.

In *The Return*, you write: "The only place I feel completely at home is in this scalding water that warms my bones." The protagonist even sleeps in the bathtub.

It starts with him reading Césaire in the bath, and it ends in a hammock, beneath apricot trees, in the paradise of the Caribbean Indians. From the tub to the hammock. It's not a metaphor. It's not a manner of speech. It's something physical. I have the impression of being a man lying prone. Always a bit of a dreamer. I think that's where the essence is, in that activity of the senses. The essence lies in the immobility that constitutes the saying I love most, that I cite most often, that of Heraclitus: "The sleeper constructs the universe."[9]

---

9   The quote cited, in French, is *"L'homme qui dort construit l'univers."* Looking up that quote in the works of Heraclitus the Obscure is a satisfying exercise that sheds light on the mechanisms of translation. Philip Wheelwright's 1959 version is "Even sleepers are workers and collaborators in what goes on in the universe." The current Penguin Classics edition of the *Fragments* has it as "Even a soul submerged in sleep is hard at work, and helps make something of the world." (Translated by Brooks Haxton, 2001). The

This is the precise area where you constructed a universe in your first book. The plot revolves around two friends discussing art and philosophy in a tiny dump of an apartment. Anyone who spent their formative years in Montreal can relate to the idea of living with another person in a space that's too small while doing questionable things in the heat of summer.

That first book, I have to admit, is a factory of fantasies of all kinds. Not necessarily sexual, but fantasies of life. People living without means have told me that, as they read the book, they had the impression they were actually living like princes. It's a bit of an eroticization of the will. The glory of poverty is that rich people can't experience it; they're prevented from doing so by their possessions. Some readers notice the evocation of freedom and liberty in the book, but many don't notice it—they see only stories of sex.

There is *some* sex—the protagonists seek to hook up with white McGill students, and they can hear their neighbours fornicating noisily at all hours, and Kant's *Critique of Pure Reason* gives them hardons—but it isn't pornographic.

---

quote cited by Laferrière appears to stem from Ferdinand Lassalle's 1857 German-language treatise on the dark philosopher of Ephesus, for in an 1889 footnote, G.T.W. Patrick renders Lassalle's German translation as "The sleeping make their own world."

There are three pages of sex, in fact. But it's imbued with sensuality.

Your English translator, David Homel, told me that your books "create an atmosphere of vibrating sexual energy without anything actually happening." It's an interesting contrast with what a reviewer at *Le Nouvelliste* once wrote: "Laferrière is totally without respect for any kind of sexual morality."

I've always loved that someone once wrote of Choderlos de Laclos's *Les liaisons dangereuses*, and the scandal that provoked, that it gave its century its bad reputation. ("*Ce livre a fait la mauvaise réputation de son siècle.*") I would take all the articles that have been published about me, all the dissertations, all the critical pieces—I would give them all just to have a phrase like that. But really the fundamental key to *How to Make Love* is the idea of freedom, in many ways. The freedom to read when you want to read. To have books, without having a lot of books. It's someone who has a couple of books on their table and who speaks of them as though he owned the library of the world. It's someone who sees the floor move because there are cockroaches, and who doesn't make a big deal about it, who doesn't start freaking out. It's someone who looks into their empty fridge and does a song of poverty, of sobriety. That's liberty. It's someone who doesn't have any food and says, *Chic! I don't need to go on a diet*. Who has to ask themselves what they'll do when they have to choose between eating and buying a book. It's not a bad question, after all. *Do I need to eat, or to buy a book?* It's better than spending your time asking yourself: *Do I need to throw out the rest of the food or eat it?* So it's someone who asks themselves questions. The themes that dominate in the book are solitude and freedom. And friendship as well. And the freedom that only those who live in a place where they weren't born can enjoy.

Tell me about that freedom.

That freedom is often spoiled because people spend their time complaining that they can't find what they left behind. Whereas the narrator in that book says, "The fact of being in a place we don't know, where we can't situate ourselves—it's a dream! We are in a dream." And in a dream, we do what we want. We feel what we want to feel. We are the master of our senses. We have the right. We dream what we want to dream. I speak a lot about sleeping in *How to Make Love*. There are female characters who fall asleep and wake up in Senegal. It's the notion of changing your life, and being conscious of doing so. We can do that in the city we live in. That's what provoked people, its subversiveness. Is it sex, or is it someone who tries to take pleasure in arriving in a new city? His mother isn't there, so he has fun. Ultimately, it's the autobiography of a dandy.

Did you consider yourself a dandy at that point? Or now?

It wouldn't be very dandy to consider oneself a dandy! A real dandy isn't someone who turns himself into a dandy. It's someone who discovers pleasure in a certain situation. Hemingway said that courage is grace under pressure. For me, that's also a way of thinking about dandyism. Courage is finding yourself somewhere, in a place, in a moment, where you shouldn't be and seeing how you react. A dandy is someone who is startled by reacting in a way and who says, *I'm acting in reality the way I would act in a dream*. I experienced that moment during the earthquake in Haiti. I faced the question everyone has to face: what will you do in the face of death? How will you behave? Will you do what you always do? Or will you panic completely? Will you be a pillar for others, or will you try to blame them? How will you behave? At that time, I had the sensation that, not just I myself, but everyone in Port-au-Prince, behaved impeccably. I come from a town that really deserves its name. They are princes there. It's rare to see people take just forty-eight hours to pick themselves up after a catastrophe that kills 300,000 people. It took them two days. And since then, there has been no progress. That's to say, people remained the same. In my case, I started writing a book. I didn't do anything personal or individual. I acted like any *Port-au-Prince-ien*, each according to their tastes, their inclinations. Elegance in difficult moments. Grace under pressure.

You started to write as soon as the earthquake happened.

Yes, right after the first tremors. It's all in *The World Is Moving Around Me*. He starts to write right away. And I started with a poetic instinct. The first thing I did was go to see if the flowers in the hotel courtyard were broken. They had long stems, and after I saw all the buildings that had collapsed, I wanted to see if they were broken, too. And not a single flower was broken. When I saw that, I recognized I'd had a poetic intuition at that supremely terrifying moment. What helped me survive was going to see if the flowers had fallen or not. It's an extravagant idea, but so fundamental to my aesthetic. And it isn't linked to a love of flowers. It's fundamental. If the flowers survived, I thought the people there would survive. The concrete had crumbled, but the flowers survived. For me, the concrete, the heavy, it's stupidity. And the flower is what permits us to float, to not break, to not shatter.

Does this connect to the idea of dandyism, to the idea of courage being grace under pressure?

Yes, this is what's so important to me about the idea of dandyism. Because we can always dream whatever we want. If they tell you that Montreal will disintegrate in ten minutes, the whole city will crumble, with everything inside of it, hundreds of thousands of deaths, and hundreds of thousands injured on top of that—what will you do? Nobody can say. It's happened to me. I saw my town fall. And I saw how people behaved, and that's maybe when I had a moment of experiencing the act of birth. I saw that I come from that town and those people. Because I behaved as they did. It's not dandy to do anything different. It's dandy because I did what they did, they who acted at the extreme point of grace. As Hemingway saw it. It's also called sangfroid. Each person tried to save everyone else, to save whatever could be saved, or whatever was around them. Instead of a panic in which each tried to find their own family, which would seem normal and instinctual, people said things like, "I hope that someone is doing for my family what I'm doing here for others."

4: THE WRITER'S ENEMY

In his *Paris Review* interview, Hemingway was asked what he thought about the idea of being politically engaged as a novelist. He said he had no problem with being a political writer, but that "All you can be sure about in a political-minded writer is that if his work should last, you will have to skip the politics when you read it." It stops being relevant.

Yes, that's it. It's as simple as that. For me, being political is speaking about literature. It's writing books. It's being available and free, meeting people, travelling. Politics for me means drawing in a neat way the figure of a writer. For me a writer is the most subversive being, the most interesting. They are in this moment what priests used to be throughout history, these beings that were paid by the population to speak about spirituality. Whether we like it or not, I've always liked the figure of the priest.

What is it that you find interesting about priests?

A priest is a *type* who is financially covered, who lives tax-free. He's there, and all we ask him to do is speak about the soul three times per day, hold mass, take care of church affairs, hold rituals. People die, and he goes into their homes and greets the family. He blesses the children that are born, he marries people. I always found that it's one of society's best inventions, to create trades or groups that are completely removed from time, removed from the present, removed from urgency. To me, the writer is the modern embodiment of that.

In a secular way?

It's more secular, yes, because we are no longer a society dominated by faith, except perhaps in the Middle East, which is increasingly so. In the West, we're no longer ruled by faith. The writer has to fill that need. And to do it well, he cannot endorse others. He has to have a deep understanding of the force of that spiritual function, so that he cannot take on any other functions. For me, a writer who is too engaged politically is a writer who has forgotten the energy that came over them when they wrote their first big book. When you've seen someone persist in that battle—Melville's white whale, *The Old Man and the Sea*, *Les misérables*—if you become too engaged in the concrete realities of politics, it's because you've forgotten that energy. That energy, it takes a life to get to the point where you've made something that contains that energy. And that absolute quality, you can find it in a book from any century, you open it, and you find that same energy. That, to me, takes a lifetime. For me, a writer who engages politically is a writer who doubts their own talent. Because they should have the talent to touch everyone everywhere at all times.

But you have to doubt your talent, don't you?

The engagement in writing is so profound, and requires so much energy, that it should take all of our mental, psychological, and aesthetic faculties. If we see that we have time to do other stuff, it's that we're no longer in it. If we feel we have to do other work to be part of our age, it means we've dropped it. In that case, it's better to drop literature and go completely into the other role. Because your writing will disappear like the others. You know it, deep down, when you are no longer putting your life into a sentence. And when you know that, you should do something else. Even if you're really talented. It's lost time, because it will erase itself, it will sink. And we aren't lacking books. That's not what's lacking. There are enough books out there to get us through to the time when the next batch of dinosaurs goes extinct.

But I imagine that you have had moments of doubt. All writers have doubts.

That's inside of the writing. There's only doubt at the core of writing. It's strange, I don't have many doubts, because I seem to be speaking here as though literature was resting on eternity. And that's not the way I write. That's not what I'm talking about. I'm not saying, "Don't write if you aren't a genius." Not at all, *au contraire*. Writing itself is linked to doubt, it moves forward that way. It's an engine that advances by explosion. There's a moment when the motor is stalled and we write a sentence and, boom—it's back on. It nourishes itself on doubt. We can't write without doubting the very universe to begin with, our own universe, our own reality, our own writing itself. That's within the system. I'm saying if you really believe you can do something else better, do it.

To get back to this idea of the writer as priest, as a person who speaks about the idea of spirituality and the state of the soul—are you a spiritual person?

No! I mean yes, certainly, like everyone else that is. Otherwise there wouldn't be any readers, we wouldn't listen to any music. That spirituality is a kind of eternity. We are in a total materiality and yet at the same time we have a need for spirituality that has nothing to do with God or religion. Spirituality is a leap beyond the present moment. We are jumping, right now, we're leaving... Let's say we have a very serious problem, a sick child. We meet our friend and we tell them our problem. We could be in Haiti, we have no medicine, no money. But then our friend tells us a story, and we start to laugh. For me, that's spirituality. We start laughing. We leave the present moment, which is completely intense, and then brusquely, we have the impression that there's another space in which we can laugh, which also means that all our problems are ephemeral. As though we were instantly transported forty years into the future. In forty years, we will have lost our grandparents, or parents, we will have known death, and got over it. It's as though we are lifted out in that peal of laughter, by that peal of laughter. That's what I call spirituality.

Laughter is spirituality?

When we pick up a book, when someone says, "I have

a problem and I picked up a book and I'm leaving the present moment," that's what I mean. It's got nothing to do with any specific kind of subject. You can choose any type of book you want, a detective story, a novel, a fable. It's totally up to you. The idea of the writer who replaces the priest, it's the idea of the intelligence of human beings who believe that, despite everything, we need to maintain that function, that poetry, that capacity, and that people can do it, full time. Books, poetry, music don't have a concrete utility—but they're so important to a society.

Is that idea of not having a concrete utility essential to art? Or *can* art have a concrete utility?

I don't know. That's the big debate, has been for a long time. I'm inside of it, and I haven't been able to reach a conclusion on it. But we'd be mistaken to believe that a beautiful sentence doesn't serve as a driving force in this society. Whether you're a writer or an artist, those who think they need to add an action to their words are mistaken, because the text itself is already an action. And if you don't think a sentence is already an action, then this isn't the right craft for you. No matter how talented you may be, this isn't your craft. And that's where politics, power, and dictators come in. The great dictator is like the great artist: he dreams of creating harmony, as a cinematographer or conductor might. He wants a harmonious society in which nobody protests. But instead of being the conductor of an orchestra, he wants to do something concrete. A novelist does the same thing: he organizes everything in his story's world, he directs that space—except that he has no authority over the object he's working on.

Are you saying there's a dictatorial side to your own writing?

Yes, there *is*… and that's why you have to avoid allowing it to enter into reality. You have to be careful to not use it to enter into society. I'm not saying we shouldn't be involved, but rather that the action of writing itself is so powerful that it creates its own movement. Literature is an action within itself, an enormous and powerful action. The writer is part of reality. To enter into political action is to leave the frame of art. If you're a painter, you paint. In writing, as soon as you start to doubt the power of writing in and of itself, as a total action that is absolute and complete, you should follow another passion.

Your books tend to explore boundary states and barriers. And you are often between worlds yourself. Reading you, it can be hard to tell if you are the narrator, or the author, or something else entirely. It's not exactly clear. In your life as well, you inhabit a variety of worlds, between Haiti and Montreal, between Paris and Montreal, between Miami and Montreal.

I write the way I live, perhaps. I don't know. I do like to cross borders. I've been doing it almost without interruption for thirty years now. I define myself that way, as someone who crosses borders. That's why I wanted to be a writer. I think the idea of the writer is also that of being able to eventually master the material, for example by being invited all over the world without needing to pay for anything. For me, the writer's enemy is money. I believe that literature can eliminate and erase money.

How so?

I'm invited everywhere and I've never paid for a hotel room or an airplane ticket. For thirty years now, I haven't paid for a single thing. That was for me the promise of literature: to make money disappear. It's an attack on the concrete. And things worked out, because I wrote books. I'm about to embark on travels right now: I'm going to be doing six or seven trips all over the world in the next two months. Everything is paid for, everything is covered. If I ever say, "I won't be able to do it, it will need to be changed by a day"— everything gets changed. And that's it. I don't abuse it. I just do it. And I don't think it's a privilege. It's the order of things. It's that priestly function again. I don't deal with money. And people know that I also have to dispense that spirituality now. You have to give back to them, so that they can feel it. That's the deal. My first book came out in 1985. Thirty years, and I travel once a month, and I don't ever have to pay for the plane tickets. I can't even use all the points I've accumulated. I can't even travel for myself because I'm invited to places so frequently.

Do you ever take a trip for yourself?

When I want to take a trip for me, I get in the car and I drive to Sherbrooke. I can't do that abroad. But for me, that's literature. Being invited to foreign countries is what I wanted. It was the promise of literature: to allow me to cross borders and to make money vanish.

And how did you make that leap? After 1976, when you first arrived here in Montreal, you had to work odd jobs to survive and also find the time to write. How did you do it? It must have taken a lot of courage to say, *I'm going to launch myself into another context.*

I didn't leap at all! I was a worker, yes, but to me I was a writer who had a job as a worker. I said to myself, "Ooh la la, what a learning opportunity." It was very important for me to be a worker. I worked at a radio station in Haiti as well, and I also had a very small salary from *Petit samedi soir*, a newspaper there. In fact, they didn't pay us in money, they gave us copies of the paper that we had to sell ourselves in order to be paid. I found a guy to sell them for me and we split the proceeds. I guess I have a strange rapport with money. The worst job I ever had in Haiti was at a bank.

A bank?

I had no idea what a bank even was. Banks are wary of poor people; I was the opposite. So I quickly gained a reputation among poor people and prostitutes as the cashier to see. There was always a lineup of people to meet with me because they'd heard that I didn't need to see any paperwork. My guiding principle was that poor people don't cheat. It wasn't a romantic idea— it's simply too complicated for them to cheat, they can't cheat a bank. Only rich people can cheat the bank. And in the whole time I worked at the bank, I never had a single problem, or bounced check, or bad deposit. They would come and deposit or withdraw their tiny sums with their bank book. All the prostitutes from the crossroads would come see me to send money to the Dominican Republic to their families and children. Those people never cheated. But because I wasn't a good banker, I never managed to balance my own numbers. It always took me so long that I'd end up going home late in the evenings, well after everybody else had checked out. As a result, they had to pay me overtime for those extra hours, so I ended up making almost as much money as the bank's director. All because they didn't understand how incompetent I was. Finally, somebody realized that it was my own fault, so they stopped paying me overages. But it was an early example of my relationship with money. If you don't know how to do things properly, I learned, you will be paid better than those who know how to do it and who will go home on time.

That is a classic Laferrière life lesson.

First, you need to not do things. Second, you need to not know how to do things. By writing and by being outside of the concrete and physical present time and by not trying to make any money, I became the person who made the most. Like if you add up all the plane tickets and hotel rooms in the world's biggest cities, it would cost a fortune for me to have done all this. And I feel the same thing in my relationship with time. Whenever you divest yourself of needs, you are immediately richer. You become freer as well. I don't need to talk about money because I can live off whatever. I can live off very little, off tea. I don't like discussing money, but abstract concepts interest me. Money turns you into a slave to money. It gives you a presence in the world, in the concrete world, and it gives you an obligation to use it, to satisfy yourself with it physically. It's connected to the body. And me, given my vision of priestly spirituality, I have to be above all that. That's the way it is for me. Somewhere between priestliness and a kind of aristocracy. We have to surpass those notions to enter directly into things. And that's why I speak of making money disappear, in order to enter into that spirituality.

It's an extremely poetic notion. I can see why people in your neighbourhood liked it when you worked at the bank. There's something magical about your way of thinking about money—about making it disappear. It's illogical but beautiful, and I do see how much sense it makes. Still, I can also imagine a banker from North America hearing it and saying, *Okay! I'm not investing in Dany.*

I don't believe in the action of receiving money. Money is not a countable energy that interests me. A dope fiend who can sell a painting for $60,000 without even finishing it is a dead man. If Basquiat hadn't been able to sell his paintings, he'd still be alive. Someone like Picasso understood that you need to manage it over time. You say, "Okay, I'll erase my vices because I want a lifelong contract. I don't want temporary power. I want a contract for life." That's how I see money, how I see basic needs. You need to eliminate money because money converts things and resolves your primary needs. If I had money myself, for example, if I myself had spent the money I made by selling books, I would've gone on trips. And that would have prohibited me from writing, because I write a lot while travelling. A person who pays for their own hotel gets up at 8 a.m. in order to see the city they're visiting. Whereas me, I never visit. I always tell the people who invite me that I don't visit. Don't give me tips on things to see, don't suggest museums, don't tell me about historic sites. I don't visit. Why not? Because I don't pay. And because I'm not paying for it, I don't care—whether I'm in the bathtub or in the bed. I'll visit another time, in another place.

So you write while you're travelling?

Absolutely.

In the hotel, at cafés, where?

In the hotel mainly. If it's for an article, I can do it in a café as well. I'll go in a corner and take some notes.

And you write in bed?

In bed, yes. In the bathtub. In the bed. Also walking around, wherever I may be, in a notebook.

And how do you transcribe those notes? No longer with your Remington 22, as with your early novels— the Remington that used to belong to Chester Himes?

No, no more Remington. By hand. And on the computer. I take notes by hand, sketching out what I'll be writing. It can be quite detailed. I think by hand. *I'm gonna talk about this: 1, 2, voilà. Then A, from 1, then B, from 2.* I do that in the bathtub, with my notebook in hand, I think, I dream. And when I'm full of that, I start writing into the computer. At that point, I forget all the notes. The notes aren't there for me to follow them. They're to give things a coherence. I need to find some coherence, and then I can get delirious again.

5: WORKING IN THE BATHTUB

Tell me more about what it was like when you first arrived in Montreal. What did you do, what sort of jobs were you able to find?

I did all sorts of jobs. I was at the airport, doing maintenance work from midnight to 8 a.m. I also worked as a janitor in a mall downtown, during those same hours. And then I had a really hard job in Valleyfield making rugs out of cows. We had to operate a kind of guillotine to cut their heads off. The cows arrived from Alberta. They were dead, but we had to cut the meat from the skin and cut the heads off their bodies. My job was to remove their skin. A cow is heavy, with all its flesh. I'd put its head under the guillotine, and then skin it. It had to be done really fast—I nearly lost an arm. Some people wanted me to get my arm cut off also, because the guy I replaced lost his arm and my co-workers were sure that if two people lost limbs they'd have to replace the machine, which was slightly defective. I also worked for one of those companies that sends people to do a different job every day and they take a cut of your salary.

A temp agency?

Yeah, that's it. They sent me everywhere. I worked in factories, doing mechanical work, assembling wooden boxes that got sent to Italy. I did a lot of things in between 1976 and 1986, when I got my first real job, working in television.

You became a weather presenter, right?

As soon as I published my first novel, I got hired as a TV weather presenter. It would seem like the question was: *How did I feel doing that? How did I have the courage to do that?* But no, I was a writer, in my head. I was a writer learning life, who was working.

Actually, I have another question: is it true you presented the weather report in the nude?

Yes, yes. I also told people that if they wanted to know the weather, they should just open the window. But for me, it was all an opportunity. I worked, I observed, I took note of how people are. I know what it takes to work physically, with your hands, and to make very little money. I was basically an illegal alien, so I wasn't paid properly. I didn't have any papers yet. I hadn't been granted refugee status, officially. I had a tourist visa, but I'd been here for years. I wasn't allowed to leave the country. I couldn't go to New York. I had no health insurance. I got that, later on, but I didn't have it then. As soon as I got my official refugee papers, which gave me resident status, they also gave me health care, and then I was able to find jobs that were a little more interesting.

Wasn't it hard to write? You say that you were always a writer, but you were working between midnight and 8 a.m. How did you find the time to write?

I didn't. I read. But yes, I was always a writer—I never wavered from that condition. I wasn't a worker—I worked in a factory, but in my head I hadn't changed my calling. I still wrote a little bit. My life was really good. Sure, when I got off work in the morning, it was something to adapt to. But I wasn't in a state where I was saying, *I need to find a space to write in.* No, I was fully immersed in my work life. And I did what I could afterwards. I read, I saw friends. I was deep in the job world, but I knew that it would feed my writing.

And it gave you the money that you needed to live. I can't imagine it was an enormous amount.

Not at all.

But at a certain point, you extricated yourself from that reality, of working at the airport and in factories, and you started writing in earnest.

Yes, at a given moment, I started... But no, I always worked on writing. What happened is that I started to understand, to take on habits, to know how to do it a little more. To know when you have to sleep, how and when to wake up. How to say to people that at certain times you are busy, that they can't just come over anytime. Nobody cares that you're working nights. But I got organized and I got started. I began writing a first book, called *The King Salomon Star Hotel*, which was the name of a hotel near my school when I lived in Haiti, where I always saw itinerant rural salesmen passing through, and *tonton macoutes*, prostitutes, government spies. Something about that hotel made an impression on me. It was in a working-class area, but it had been a nice hotel at one point. The neighbourhood became too poor, but someone still operated this low-grade hotel that had an armoire with a nice wedding dress inside. It was the idea of looking into that brothel, which was a whole world to me, a universe. I'd always wanted to write about that, and then I did—and then I lost it.

You lost it?

I moved, and I put it in some boxes on the street, and someone brought beer over, and we drank the beer and forgot about the boxes. When we remembered, they were gone. The garbage truck had come and taken the boxes away – we looked everywhere for them, in the garbage trucks, but they'd thrown it out, they thought it was garbage. I never found it. It was... But at the same time, I told myself that it must be for the best, because that's what allowed me to write my first novel, which was set in Montreal.

Was it painful to lose it?

No, no, no. On one hand, yes. Maybe for two or three days, but not more than that. I'm the sort of person who believes things happen for a reason. If it's lost, it's that it's supposed to be lost. I even said to myself, *This will permit me to write a book that takes place in Montreal.*

Your first book ended up being all about Montreal. While you were writing it, were you doing other work or not?

What was I doing? Little things. Yes, I worked. But at the end, I was doing lighter work. I had a job with Canada World Youth, where I taught a bit about Haitian culture. It was really poorly paid. In fact, I don't even know if they paid me or not. I don't remember, but for a while I slept there and I ate there and everything. So I definitely worked while writing *How to Make Love*—because I had to pay the rent at my apartment. And that's always the hardest thing. Food I could always figure out. I can eat very little, go to public markets at the end of the day when they're closing, parcel things out and make them last. But the rent was due every week. I stayed at places where you pay by the week back then.

Yes, you've written about the landlord's daughter.

Yes, the building owner's daughter. But there are all sorts of things that happen in life. You can't only pay with money. That's why I often talk about a young woman I met in Haiti way back when. She was a young girl who was a kind of semi-prostitute. She told me, "I'm not a prostitute." And that's maybe my definition of myself as well: I'm not a prostitute. I don't want money—but I want everything that money can buy. So he bypasses the physical presence of the object, of money, of the ticket, to head toward satisfaction.[10] He claims the satisfaction that money

---

10 Note: Laferrière apparently started speaking about himself as a character in the third person here, as he does in many

can produce instead of the money itself. It's not bad: he skips a step.

Ok, but to come back to the daughter of the building owner in Montreal. You've written about how you— or should I say he?—seduced her and slept with her in order to not have to pay rent. The same with a cashier at Pellat's grocery store, to get free food. Is that true? Did that really happen?

It both did and did not... At the same time, my life is very much that: I spend my life avoiding paying for things. Money has to become something that disappears. I spent my life looking for ways to not have to use money. Especially money that I don't have. By giving something else. I have energy to give, either in a book, or in speeches, or by attending writing festivals. I spend my life daydreaming about ways to offer myself as a solution to money. I always have to re-evaluate my own value. It can't be too low, or too high. You can't overvalue yourself. But I use the capital of the body, of the spirit, always in good faith with the person with whom I'm conducting a financial transaction. You wouldn't believe how sensitive people are to the idea of the writer.

How so?

---

of his books.

I've met people in places where I was a tenant, where they didn't force me to pay the rent, because I was a writer and they heard me writing. I lived in a place near the bus station on rue Saint-Hubert, where two older ladies who adored me gave me free meals and took care of me—because I was a writer. They didn't understand how someone who worked in a factory, who was black, an immigrant, from an extremely poor country like Haiti, could want to be a writer. And could also take it seriously. Could take his money, buy some books, and stay in his room and read. I really spent that period there living without knowing how money circulates. This is the first time that I really discuss money in such an organized way, actually.

I'm enjoying it.

This really gets to the heart of energy, and the spiritual question, which is to say the question of how to bypass the intermediary at the core of power dynamics, money itself. It's not what money produces in terms of satisfactions that I'm contesting, nor what you can buy with it. It's simply money itself that causes problems. The more you want to possess it, the less chance you have of possessing it. When I think of everything I've had—all the plane tickets, hotel rooms, meals, soirées—it all happened because I didn't ask for money. As soon as you start counting, you're under its influence.

It must have been quite precarious being a young writer attempting what you attempted with that book.

I don't know. I wrote the book, and sometimes I wasn't satisfied with things and then I'd keep going. I worked. I did my journalism, and I made a little money, and I wrote and I read and I wasn't too stressed out about things. I wasn't stressed out because I knew I was a reader, and I knew I would always be able to read. And I wasn't in much of a rush either. I wrote and I knew it was different from what other people were writing, I knew Montreal had never been described that way, that this was something new. It was a character talking about Montreal without hiding their true nature, a reader, a man who knows the city. We weren't in the ghetto, we weren't into nostalgia for the country left behind, and we weren't in a slum in the newly adopted homeland. And racism wasn't the centre of the book either. Because of the title, I knew I'd get into it. But it didn't end up being a frontal racism. It was a hedonistic racism, which is to say a celebratory one.

Hedonistic racism? Celebratory racism?

The character is thrilled to be misunderstood, to be looked down upon. He comes off as a young Negro, but then you speak with him and he can talk about Marguerite Duras, James Baldwin, Gabrielle Roy,

Hölderlin, Patricia Highsmith, Leonard Cohen, Norman Mailer, the Koran, Charlie Parker, Sigmund Freud. And he can speak about it all with a sense of detachment. It's as though he's a character who is mocking himself, who says, *From afar, you can see me as a Negro, but when you get closer you'll be ashamed to not believe that this young man can be so rich.* Kind of like with any young person, when people say, *Bah, young people can't read or write.* And then when you start speaking with them you realize they're actually quite cultured. They just don't feel the need to say it out loud, to declare it. And then you feel bad that you misjudged them.

You wanted the book to be misjudged?

I saw it as being similar to Basquiat. At first it just seems like graffiti, but then you see all the traces of western culture within the images: you see Leonardo da Vinci, you see Picasso, but drawn with very contemporary lines, as though he was tagging. That's what I tried to do with the book. You get close to the character and you realize when you try to tell him what Picasso is that he not only knows what it is—he knows it better than you do. Plus he connects it back to Leonardo da Vinci. That's what I wanted to do. I wasn't in a hurry.

You say you knew you were a reader, that you would always be able to read. Do you prefer to read or to write?

One engenders the other. I write because I have read. And I write because I like people to know things, because of what I've read. The writers I love are writers who read. They're writers who talk about the books they've loved. Borges, Henry Miller, Montaigne. They all talk about their readings. It can go either way for me. I love reading. I could have spent my life without writing, just reading. And I don't think I could have spent my life writing, without having read. I don't see it. Since I began I've always been a reader. Always.

While living in Paris, you've started publishing handwritten *romans dessinés*, illustrated novels. The first one was entitled *Autoportrait de Paris avec chat* or *Self-portrait of Paris with Cat*.

I wanted to do a book that I did not know how to do. I don't know how to draw, and my handwriting is terrible, so I thought, *Why not do a book about Paris?* Somewhere between imaginary and real, as I usually do, but drawn and written by hand.

It came out in 2018. And there have been two more illustrated novels since then.

L'exil vaut le voyage (*Exile Is Worth the Trip*) was published on March 18, 2020, during the height of Coronavirus pandemic. So it came out when bookstores were shuttered, including independent bookstores, which is where my readers tend to shop. My previous illustrated book, *Vers d'autres rives* (*Toward Other Shores*), came out on the day that Notre-Dame caught fire in Paris in 2019. One could say that I've been having bad luck. But that's not my view of literature. For me, a book is not a product that expires; it can be reborn from its ashes at any moment. And a good book is always relevant. I hope that both of those books are good books. In any case, I put everything into them that I could from the bottom of my belly. They are books of the belly regardless of the lyricism of the drawings and the colours.

What are they about?

L'exil vaut le voyage was born of the fact that I've always resisted the parallel that gets drawn so frequently between exile and pain. Granted, there's some pain in exile, but not every day, and we can also feel great joy living abroad. It can allow us the possibility of voyaging through others.

You talk in the book, as you so often do, of journeying via books, of travelling alongside writers, by reading them. What about *Vers d'autres rives?*

It's the preparation for the journey. Life in the home country. The author makes a cultural inventory of everything that shaped them: the poetry, the paintings, the vivid images of childhood. They put all of that in a big pot to make a good meal, as their grand-mother used to do in the kitchen. These *tableaux*, which are sketched, croquis drawings, are similar to the Haitian primitive paintings done by illiterate artists whose sophistication recalls this haiku by Bashō:

The rice-planting songs
Of the far northern peasants
First lesson in style.[11]

Why did you want to start including drawings in your books?

---

11 Bashō, like Heraclitus, is famously daunting to translate. The pivot words in his haikus have multiple possible meanings and implications, and were intended to sow ambiguity. (No wonder Laferrière admires him so much.) He quoted the following French version of the poem, which I then rendered in English in haiku form:

Les chants de repiquage
Des paysans du nord
Première leçon de style.

This is Noboyuki Yuasa's 1966 translation, from the original Japanese:

The first poetic venture
I came across—
The rice-planting songs
Of the far north.

And the following is Sam Hamill's 1998 translation:

Culture's beginnings:
From the heart of the country
Rice-planting songs.

It's something that goes way back for me, to my childhood. I remember at the end of the school year, in July, they'd give back our exercise books and let us do whatever we wanted with them. I turned them into kites. It was such a joy to strip the homework notebooks of their function. It made me happy. It's the same pleasure I feel in returning to childhood to begin with, and in doing something new, something we don't often see. I'd never seen books like this before. There's an entire library of hand-written, illustrated books, but *drawn* books that aren't picture books, nor graphic novels, are quite rare. I wanted to tell the same sorts of stories I always tell, but in another form.

Do you still hope to one day write a cookbook, as you mentioned to me several years ago?

All my ideas stay with me for a long time before seeing the light of day. What's important is that an idea needs to find its place in the structure that I've been building for almost 40 years. I need to be able to link each book project to at least two other books. For the moment, there's not yet a book of recipes, but you can find a lot of examples of cooking in my books. My characters like eating a lot, and I like to make them food.

You also made a fantastic meal of Haitian *legim* once, when I came over to your home. Would you mind sharing that recipe here?

My recipe for *aubergine à l'étouffée*, in Creole, is called *touffé bérégène*. It's made with eggplant, pork, carrots, onion, a head of lettuce, a bit of tomato sauce, salt, garlic, pepper, and chilli pepper. Everything goes into a big stockpot. You can either cook the meat separately, well spiced, and then add it at the end, or you can start out with the meat and then add the vegetables to it. It all gets mixed up together in the pot with some boiling water and spices. This is exactly the same as my writing methodology.

The Laferrière gumbo, where everything blends together—memories, imagination, dreams, advice, literary reflections—into a harmonious word stew.

Music plus emotion equals rhythm. And rhythm is the foundation of poetry. I've been hearing that same rhythm for such a long time, and that's what determines my style.

There is a palpable musicality to your work in French. That rhythm may be why it's a challenge to translate your work into English. It's the impossibility of translating any poetic work.

My books are only held together by the grace of poetry. That's all that interests me.

You've said, in speaking about Haitian poets you love, that it's the obligation of less well-known writ-

ers to help more accomplished writers who deserve
to be read on a wider scale. Can you clarify that idea
for us?

I always think about that. To be precise, it has to do
with bartering, and of diffusing energy. Meaning
that when you've read a writer you like, you have to
do your utmost to help them become better known,
in your own circle. That's part of the literary econ-
omy, that idea. There's nothing charitable or Chris-
tian about it; it's just about spreading the word about
someone you think is better than you. Helping another writer become known is even more important than writing. And it ensures you don't fall into
narcissism, too. Which may be why certain writers
who can't do it themselves turn to translation. Even
if we don't do translation, we can still talk about a
writer. We can read their work in public. We can talk
about them. That's what I've done in my books: I
speak often about other writers. There's a profusion
of them. I'm always speaking about writers, painters, musicians, always. That's part of the reason that it
isn't autofiction, or fictionalizing myself. It's a group
autofiction. When I write about a writer I like and
then someone says, *Hey, I didn't know about that artist
and now I'm quite happy to know them,* at that moment,
I feel as though I maybe wrote that author's books.
I was the one who wrote that! It's a Borgesian idea also.
He said that what is good belongs to translation, to
language itself. What is good is us. It's you. For me,

making a big writer become more renowned is a good way of actually being a big writer. The big writers *are* you. It's simple, help them out. You read them and you make it known that you've read them. Borges always had that vision. He liked the verb "to legitimize." It can legitimize a life to raise people's awareness about someone we find interesting, important, someone bigger than ourselves.

That's a beautiful idea.

Borges taught me about so many writers, French writers, all the great classic British writers, Locke, also Kant, Schopenhauer. I learned so much from him about Sarmiento, and Hernandes, the Argentine poet he admired so much. And so many different literatures as well: Scandinavian, Irish, Spanish, the sagas, Icelandic novels from the 12th and the 14th centuries. He sees science fiction as a version of theology, so he makes you aware of theology, cinema, westerns, music, the milonga, the tango. He makes you aware of so much. It's a universe that's made up of everything in the world. He used to say that originality is a modern superstition. Everybody wants to be original; instead of trying to be original, we should just try to make what already exists better known.

6: A TERRIBLE APPETITE FOR LIFE

Family is so important in your writing.

My father was a political activist and a dandy. My mother used to say that he would change shirts twice or three times a day, at least. He always dressed in white. And my mother—she was always very discreet, timid, but at the same time determined, because she had to put up with my father.

Tell me a bit about your mother's determination. Is that something that passed down into your DNA that allowed you to have published as many books as you have.

Yes, there is that. But I think I took something from both of them. My father was determined as well, but in an explosive way. My mother was determined, but in a discreet way. I'm a mix of the two. My mother is more contemplative, and my father was more a man of action. He became the mayor of Port-au-Prince at a very young age. And my mother was someone with values, who valued family above all else, and the cohesion of the family. She always tells me to go see my aunts. Whenever she writes me a letter, it's the first thing she says. And she always says, "Family is very important, you must never break the links." So, hers is a collective determination. I learned from her that you don't need confrontation to do what you want to do. A confrontation means that you go on to the terrain of another, who wants something from you or sees something in you. You can consider it, and if you don't want to do it, you can just continue on your way. You don't need to confront it. You don't need to say, *I don't want that path*; you simply go your own way. I got that from my mother.

Were you always that way?

I wasn't like that when I was younger, but as time goes on I see many things in a more contemplative manner. I let things go, and they take care of themselves, most of the time. All we have to do is what we ourselves have decided on. The action we want within the framework we're working within. Our next action is structured by what we've already done. I very much believe that one action engenders another. I write books, and each book that I write forms a cohesive link with the others, and that cohesion determines my future. I trust in the movement of what happens to me at this point, of the small misfortunes that happen in the context of my craft. My first book has been continuously in print for thirty years, and so I just try to follow it, because it is always present.

How so?

It has a durability, something inside it that I don't understand. I follow it like it's a pilot fish showing me the way. And when I watch time passing, all the things that have happened—some dazzling, some not dazzling—and the things that have derailed me, the only thing that never deviated was *How to Make Love*, which has continued on its path. I try to see how it integrates itself into the others, and how the others influence it. That structure is more profound than anything I could have come up with. So many years of my past, of my passions, are there. I prefer to follow them than to try to get out in front of them.

And that comes from my mother. In the past, I would have thought I need to lead, that I need to be more aggressive, that I'm the one making my way, I'm the one who did it. But now I just follow.

I think it was your mother who compared you to your father by saying that you have "a terrible appetite for life."

Ah yes, that was my mother. I'm the proof that she met my father.

His name was the same as yours: Windsor Klébert Laferrière.

Yes. My father had to flee for his life when he was exiled by Duvalier. At the time, he was Deputy Secretary of Commerce. There were big protests going on, as it was at the beginning of Duvalier's régime. To provoke protests, the big food merchants were in the habit of starving the populace by withholding merchandise. Most major protests, which could lead to the overthrow of the regime, started in the open-air markets, which were the heart, the stomach of Port-au-Prince. Anyway, my father went on radio and, sounding like a Marxist, he declared, "If the bourgeois merchants are stockpiling merchandise, the people have the right to break into shops." As Deputy Secretary of Commerce, he was the person in charge of those very shops! Advocating for looting! So they forced him into exile.

Where did he go?

He ended up in New York. He became ill. Nobody really knows what was wrong with him. Meaning, to be clear, that he lost his mind. He lost everything, and he ended up a total recluse. He walked. He would do Manhattan to Brooklyn every day, on foot. He was cut off from society, but people respected him because they considered him someone who could have done something for Haiti. That's how they talk in Haiti. He was somewhere between 26 and 30 when he left.

And how old were you when you left Haiti?

Twenty-three. I had to flee the country, too, just like him. What's different is that, when my father left, there wasn't much emigration from Haiti, so he found himself alone in New York City, living in solitude. He was a man of crowds: the Mayor of Port-au-Prince. And when I left, in 1976, there had already been enough immigration to Montreal that I found myself part of a community, an atmosphere.

You left Haiti because of the assassination of your friend, the journalist Gasner Raymond.

Yes, Gasner was my best friend. [We wrote for the same paper] and were always together. He was a militant and a subversive. He wasn't afraid of anything. He was a novelistic character, a romantic. He would tell people, "Dany and I, we know we are going to die before the age of 30." I would think to myself, *Not me*. But I couldn't tell him that because he was so enthusiastic. I was the prudent one.

In what way?

My articles didn't have sentences in code denouncing the regime. His did. He did a series on prostitution and its connection to political corruption. I wrote about literature, film, painting... But then, we did a series of articles together on the cement industry strike. We interviewed the factory workers. I knew what we were doing was extremely dangerous. The article was published. There was a picture of Gasner with the strikers. The news director hit the ceiling. I didn't understand why he was so furious. One or two weeks later, Gasner was killed. Then there were rumours that I was going to be next. So I left the country for Montreal.

You left right away?

No, there was the funeral. One or two days later, a week? I had no sense of time. Every day, every minute, you felt you were in danger. But I was there, at the funeral. I couldn't be a pallbearer, though, and I was his best friend. I had always taken one basic precaution in Haiti, which was not to get myself killed by being an idiot. I did show myself. I had to write for the newspaper. It was important to write about literature, film, and theatre. Maybe as important, or even more, important than about dreams of rebellion. In terms of rebellion, it's better to talk about an interesting movie and get people to go see it. You don't need to die. As we've discussed, for me, being political is discussing literature.

What else do you remember about your father from that time?

After time passes, you lose a lot of things. What you keep is the image, the emotion, the feelings. But you lose the physical presence.

"A star too blinding / to look at straight on. / That's what a dead father is," you wrote in *The Return*.

When my mother watches me, she'll say, "You eat like your father. You say thank you like your father. You say thank you, but it's as though you aren't thankful. It's a brief, dry 'Thank you.' And you also have that insatiable appetite for life that your father had." She says it with a note of sadness, because she sees her husband in me. And also because she's worried that that temperament will cause me to do things that will land me in difficult situations, even dangerous ones.

Tell me more about this idea of appetite. Does it reveal itself in your writing?

In everything. In the way I eat, first of all. I eat as though the food in front of me is the only thing that exists. People tell me I eat as though my life depended on it. I just thought I was eating normally. And then I realized that other people eat with a distance between themselves and the food. How can you have a distance there? What is it they're trying to control? I'm completely into whatever I'm doing. In a conversation, I'm totally present. I have the impression that time doesn't exist, even if we only have a half-hour. There's no calculation, not in the moral sense of the term. Don't count the minutes, don't count your energy, be totally in whatever it is you're doing, as though there's no hierarchy to activities. Eat with the same passion that you speak, write, walk, travel. As though you were always in the present indicative, as though everything is happening in the present.

Are your books written in the present indicative?

They are all written in the present indicative. Even the books about my childhood are written in the present indicative. It's a continual present. It's a very hot present, burning in the present indicative. It's because I find that's the only time that exists. The past is found in memory, so I don't trust memory. And the future is a hope of people who live in countries where life expectancy is very long. I was raised by my grandmother in a place where each day we looked to find what we would eat. Each day had to be lived. At the end of the day, at the moment of going to bed, we would thank the Lord for having allowed us to pass a day so full, from beginning to end: "We are not dead, we were not hungry." Because everything was complete. I wrote about this in *The Return*. We're born in the morning, we grow up at noon, and we die in the evening. And the following morning we change bodies. We take another body. All is finished in the day. It is complete. That's the present. We use our body up all the way to its limits, and then take another one next day. There's no strategy, there's no calculation for the morning after, there's no preservation of energy.

The last time I saw you speak in public, you were professing your love for "bad," cheap wine.

Literature makes that possible. In literature, we can like bad wines. The words "bad wine" are better than "nice wine." The idea of bad wine conjures all sorts of more interesting things than "good wine." It's more easy-going, less snobbish, not to mention the words "good wine" are often used falsely. Oenologists will tell you that most French people who claim to love wine can't tell the difference between a really expensive wine and a really cheap wine. So I prefer to talk about bad wine. It makes more sense to write about what you know.

Is there anything impossible in literature?

Vengeance. Vengeance is an impossible word. It's also an impossibility. It's impossible to avenge yourself. To avenge yourself means that you are still within a situation. The only vengeance that is possible is to forget the affront that has been committed, to be so satisfied in other ways that the difficulty gets erased, whatever it was. At a certain moment, the person who wronged you is still important to you and you'd like a fine to be paid, a punishment equal to the affront. But if that gets erased by other, more important things that you've done, well, then you've distanced yourself from that zone. It will become smaller and smaller, and will eventually even transform itself into a motor. You may even come to realize that it was a good thing that it happened to you, as it permitted you to get to where you are. That's vengeance. And a certain point in time, you even forget the source. A person comes up to you and says, "You don't remember me? I want to apologize."

"Apologize for what?" you ask.

"But you must remember, you came to see me when you were freaking out and penniless, and I didn't help you, even though I owed you money at the time."

And you say, "Oh that? It wasn't a big deal!" When in reality, it had been one of your greatest wounds for years. You cannot avenge yourself. Because if it continues to be serious, you are still in it, even if you say, *Look, you wronged me, but look at what I've become.* Because you're going to be hurt if they say, *Who cares?* Because that man needs to accept that you have become bigger than he aspired to be, and that the hurt he caused you is what permitted you to grow. That is his humiliation. The only way to have vengeance is to forget completely, not artificially. Our only vengeance is the number of people who've done us in that we've forgotten.

But you are a writer. Isn't there some element of vengeance that fuels the work of your writing?

There are interior fires. They don't all have a source in something negative. Or at least, I don't see it that way. I firmly believe that vengeance is not one of my interior fires. For example, I write about my family. Many writers from the third world build their literary glory on the denigration of their family. They try to build a personality that is so strong that it doesn't need anybody else to have gotten there, as though they sprang from Jupiter's thigh, self-born. They say they never had books at home, no libraries, nothing at all, no family—everything to show the effort they had to undertake, the power of their accomplishment. But I think you can have another source.

What would you say is *your* source?

My source is to have climbed as a group, to arrive grouped together. The whole group—Petit-Goâve, with my aunts—and to have made them into characters, to have somehow given back what they gave me. I always found it strange that writers thank people in their acknowledgments. I put that into the interior of my books. I'm not alone. I advance in a group formation. Portrait of the writer with a group of women. With a group of cities, even. With people I don't even know, accompanied by Montrealers. That's not a negative source. It's more like, *I'll manage to make you into beings as universal as any of the other characters in universal literature.*

Not bad.

There is no place that doesn't deserve to be literary. Many Caribbean, African, and Latin-American writers don't talk about their families, about their places. They create totally autonomous novels and worlds. All to show that the writer gives birth to himself. He is born out of his readings or born out of himself. In my case, I thought it would be interesting to show universal literature that I am not born exclusively from readings of books from abroad. I am also born of the affection of my people and of my reading of that society and of my family. If I sometimes aggravate European writers because I describe a childhood that was happy under dictatorship, I tell them that they're doing the same thing when they describe their extremely unhappy childhoods. Because they can't tell it in a happy way, their spirits are constructed of acidity. André Gide said that happy feelings are not literary. Which I find false. Why can't happiness be just as valid as bad feelings? They have to write what they have to write, but I found another form. It gets repetitive in all my books, but I'm able to keep using good feelings because that isn't played out in literature yet.

So vengeance doesn't enter into that at all?

No, it doesn't enter into it. What happens, rather, is the installation of new feelings. It's a new space where I don't need to be in agreement with those who've analyzed literature and decreed that it needs to be a certain way. Literature has moments. It's a living organism. It lives with its era. And changes. There are permanent aspects, but it lives in its epoch.

7: APPROXIMATING REALITY

Let's look at that idea of literature as a living organism. In your books, there's a desire to access reality, even if you employ massive imagination to get there. You describe yourself in an extremely open and unguarded way in your books, and increasingly so in later books. *The Return* is one of your least protected books, one with the least armour. But what about the other people you describe? It can't always be easy for them to see themselves described in such an honest, unflinching way—or at least to see themselves described from your perspective. Is there cruelty in that?

There's a good-natured ambiance in my books. I'm not a writer dominated by bitterness, by acidity, even by lucidity. There's good will in all of it. And that's very important when you describe somebody. If it's done under positive auspices, you can say things that are quite clear. Almost tough things, even. And the person will accept this because they know you didn't put them in the book to gun them down. Most of the people in my books don't actually live in the places that I put them in, where the action takes place. Even so, people are usually proud to have been put into the space I've put them in. Even if they've led a disastrous life, they know I've made an effort to portray them in a nuanced way. All of that is dominated by happy things, like a cup of coffee with Da. There's no instinct in me to go and take someone I hate and pillory them in my book. I don't think that's good for the book. And it isn't good for my spirit either. I prefer to forget. Or to fix things myself, at full voice, if there's a problem. I don't solve my life problems in my books. Even if, despite everything, there are some people who get angry at the way they're depicted.

Do you ever ask them how they feel about it?

I never ask them what they think. I never ask my mother, or my aunts, or anyone at all what they think of my books. Which means I'm not troubled by any of it. I don't censor myself, nor do I seek to rectify a portrait if a person complains about the way their nose has been drawn. But I don't get a lot of complaints. Or, if I get them, it's less about the individual portraits and more about the general ambiance. That's what stays in people's heads. It's the town of Petit-Goâve, it's Port-au-Prince. It's the snow. It's freedom. It's an individual's solitude. It's desire. So I'm not at all the type of writer who describes in a way that provokes excessive reactions. Plus, whatever I do, I do to my family, to my mother, to my aunts, and above all to myself.

But you can be so intense with yourself, or with the "you" that is a character. You're somewhere in between those two things in your books—sort of yourself, sort of a version of yourself. That must sometimes be difficult for others, for those around you.

Yes, but I don't want to know about it. I think it has to be done that way and it's good for the book. It's the book that is like that, that demands that the person be described. Those who are close to me, either they don't read or, if they do read, they get it. They're reading a novel. My wife, for example, knows she's reading a novel. She never seeks to find me in my books because she knows. She's been living with me since 1979, after all. So she doesn't try to understand me by reading my books. She knows she needs to especially watch out when the events I'm describing seem to be most direct. She knows to watch out because she knows I don't put my energies into approximating reality.

"He who wants to be transparency itself can do nothing but hide himself and make himself obscure," as Blanchot wrote.

Realism isn't real. And the more I try to get close to myself, the more I'm hiding something. If the details seem true to life, it's because the main detail is not in fact true. And the portrait isn't either. That's why I use so many details from life. To balance that out, my wife has to look in my philosophical writings. She might actually find the real me there. A book like *The Almost Forgotten Art of Doing Nothing At All* is actually an autobiography of my emotions. And *Journal of a Writer in Pyjamas* is an autobiography of my spirit. She knows work like that is closer to the real me than the portraits in books that seem to be true to life. So, over time, she dropped the idea of trying to put a face on the portrait.

Is it hard for your family when you are writing?

You'll have to ask them. [*Dany turns to his wife, Maggie, who is in the room next to us.*] *Chérie!* Adam wants to know if it's hard for you when I'm writing.

Maggie: [*Enters, laughing.*] His writing is my rival, *quoi.* Yes, it's difficult. When he writes, he's no longer there. He closes in on himself. He's no longer there.

Does he write often?

Maggie: Yes, he's always in the middle of writing something, even if it isn't a book.

So even if he isn't actually writing…

Maggie: He's thinking. He has a little notebook where he puts all his ideas. A little black notebook. [*To Dany.*] Adam is interviewing me, I'll have you know. And he knows how to get me to talk.

Dany: And you're talking?!

Maggie: Yes, out of friendship with Linda Leith. [*To Adam.*] But you can't ever tell anybody that I spoke to you.

I won't tell anybody. I haven't heard a thing. [*Maggie exits.*] Dany, Montreal's identity can be defined by the idea that so many people here feel like they don't really belong, that it can be hard to feel a real sense of belonging here. Many francophones don't feel like they belong to this country or this continent, many anglophones don't feel like they are a part of this French-speaking society, and countless minority groups struggle to fit in. Is that something that con-

nects all of us here, that sense of not belonging? Are we all bound together by our outsiderness?

Yes, it's a kind of state of anxiety. But it's a good thing to not have the impression of being part of things. And a lot of people here have that sensation—maybe most people. So when most people share that anxiety, it's pretty interesting. It makes for a dynamic society, always looking behind itself before saying anything.

But not in a paranoid sense, I don't think.

No, just worried, just anxious. And with something to say. Because someone who belongs no longer feels a need to make a point. People here have an argument to make, they feel the need to state why they should belong and why they don't belong. But I think those questions and those debates are more of a winter thing here. In winter, we concoct things. It's an intellectual identity: we make things up in our heads, we get affronted, we confront. Whereas in summer, it's all about the body. We're satisfied just walking down the street. Space pleases us, whereas space in winter is rigorous and makes us want an enemy. I don't think anybody wants to debate in July when it's sunny out and they're eating a salad with a glass of wine on a terrasse.

Why do you think this place is the way it is?

Quebec has, for a long time, been bothered by the fact that it was colonized by the English. *Nègres blancs d'Amérique,* as Pierre Vallières put it. But more and more, Quebec seems to be accepting that it is a North American society. We have a French touch, with the language, and the culture, and the taste of France. But in our way of thinking, of talking, of feeling— we are North American. As much English-Canadian as American. Quebec is part of North America, in the end. And maybe that's why Quebec has such a passion for identity: it's a passion for saying that we're unique in North America. We're the only Roman Catholic society, the only francophones, the only ones who banished the church to create a truly secular society. It's a passion for being a *distinct society*, for being unique individuals. I'm not too sensitive to all it—or at least, I'm more sensitive to what it's like in Montreal, rather than in the broader Quebec at large. Montreal is the laboratory experiment of Quebec. And it can't quite get in line with the national identity of Quebec.

It's different, at times.

Almost opposite. Sometimes it is the actual opposite, even.

In Haiti, people aren't as obsessed with the idea of identity as they are here in Quebec.

No, they have other problems. It's a country that accepts that it's an extremely difficult place. Whereas Quebec has from the start tried to make France realize they were wrong about us: *You thought we were nothings, just ex-cons, and look! We made a real country here.* Haiti never wanted to demonstrate that. Haitians' energy goes elsewhere, toward resolving the dictatorships, toward the question of eating. As much as Haitians want their children to go to school and have access to health, I don't think that their end goal is to create an extremely comfortable society where nothing ever happens. I think that some part of the memory of being warriors, the memory of independence, lives on. The construction of the self is very strong there, and people are proud to have made it through storms and hard times. They define themselves based on their resilience. People are poor, but that doesn't mean they let others do whatever they want to them. That's the memory of the slave who has become independent through warfare. *Don't forget: I've already broken these chains before. Just because I happen to be poor doesn't change anything.*

Is there a sense in Haiti that a popular movement could at any instant radically transform things?

The country contains within its structure the fact that everyone participated in the war of independence. That's why there is often a violence to the discourse there, but it rarely translates into action. Violence there is verbal, for the most part. The actual violence in Port-au-Prince results from the fact that the city is now encircled by slums. If it weren't for the poverty all around, it would be quite a quiet city, like cities in other parts of the country.

How did you experience growing up under a dictatorship?

Living in a dictatorship meant that at certain moments of my life, my parents worried and stopped us from going out. Dictatorship felt like prohibition. You no longer have a normal existence. But let's remember that the dictatorship wasn't dictatorial 24/7. We had school, we had classes, we attended them. There was a silence. There was the sense that you can't say what you think. There was an element of palpable oppression. There were *tonton macoutes* in the street—and you had to be aware of them, and be careful. But as kids, we didn't really know about all that. We didn't know what it could be like if you spoke your mind. We weren't interested in being for or against Duvalier. Like kids everywhere, we went anywhere we wanted and did whatever we pleased. For me, being in a little rural place like Petit-Goâve was no different than it was for any other kid. I had homework. I wanted to see movies, go dancing, play. Being a child in a dictatorship, well, you're born into it, and you know you need to be careful. You still manage to live.

You've written three illustrated children's books. Is it fair to say that they echo the themes of your grown-up books?

Yes, like all of my books they are about my life. And they are also about the questions that are most important for children: love, death, and politics. Politics are pivotal to all of us, especially those who spend their childhood under a dictatorship. For me, my childhood had a lot to do with the dictatorship, with power, with the effects of power on myself. But the question of race, for example, didn't affect me at all in my childhood. Until I was 23 years old, I was in Haiti. And, again, it's not identity politics that concerns Haitians; it's really the struggle to survive.

You often write about identity—but what are your thoughts on the word "race"?

It's an anachronism, something old that is no longer really used. In a dictionary context, at the *Académie* we'd say that the word *race* is used in the sense of a group of individuals of the same skin colour. And employing that meaning is archaic. It's old-fashioned and no longer relevant. Its general usage has ceased.

Surely not everyone sees it that way?

It depends on the country. In Haiti, according to our constitution, everyone who lives there is a Negro. So there's no problem. Even if you're blond or Japanese, if you are Haitian, you're a Negro. That's that. Some of my readers may read me as a black writer, but I wasn't black for the first 23 years of my life. We are all equal under the dictator. In Montreal it's one way, in the rest of Quebec another. In France, it's complicated—and they're deeply involved in the question of identity. In America, yes, they're still in it. No group can say that the debate over race is over in America.

Does the racial war in America preoccupy you?

All wars are preoccupying. The reasons may be less preoccupying to us if we aren't directly in the war, but the fact that people are killing each other is preoccupying. The number of black Americans who are killed, or are incarcerated, is so vast that it can't be a coincidence. The consequences are absolutely preoccupying, but the reasons behind them are another question.

A theme in all of your books is the desire to make borders vanish. Is it fair to say that applies in terms of this obsolete-yet-still-extant notion of race as well?

To read me based on skin colour is to read me incorrectly. The deep question that has always concerned me is the question of freedom, individual freedom. And intimacy. As you point out, a more precise way to read me has to do with dissolving borders—and, even more than erasing borders, with celebrating movement and mobility across the entire world. Certain people want to assign things to you, and think they can have opinions of you before they know you. That bothers me. It affects yellow and red and white and other people as well. All literature is made precisely to find out what we are. It's a discovery—but it's a useless discovery, because everyone finds themselves in the same predicament. We all come from a place where we were born, we all have a rapport with childhood, and what happened then, and all of that impacts how we write.

While preparing for this interview, I hadn't even thought of discussing race with you—it was actually my editors at *The Paris Review* in New York who read an early draft of our conversation and were puzzled that we hadn't gotten into the subject.

That's because they are American. It would be more noteworthy if we didn't discuss it—if we didn't feel the need to discuss it. I wrote a book about this, called *Je suis fatigué* [*I Am Tired*]. It's all about how tired I was of being seen as a Caribbean writer, as a Québécois writer, as an ethnic writer, as an exiled writer—instead of just simply as a writer. We all know nationalist cultures are boring. I believe the reason you never brought it up is because you know me.

But I only really know you the way any of your readers knows you.

That's right.

And yes, in reading you, I often have the sense that we end up sharing the same mind, the same thoughts, the same dreams.

That's precisely it. That's what I try to do with all my books. When I say I'm a Japanese writer, that's just one side of me. I move! I don't move to avoid problems; I keep moving because I'm a mobile type. A moving target. I move under the earth, I move in the water, I move through the air. I move I move I move. I move because I don't want to get caught and stuck and pinned anywhere, no matter what the place may be. *Je bouge.*

In *Journal of A Writer in Pyjamas* you write of how, at the outset, you were aware that suffering plays a part in writing and that literature requires struggling and pain—but you decided that it wouldn't be like that for you. Was that decision based on the experiences you had in Haiti, or in the factories you worked at here, the ones where "the mornings are always grey and the skies always low?"

And the summers really nice, also. But yes, I heard writers speaking on the radio about the pain of writing, and I always thought they were exaggerating their suffering, that they were laying it on a little thick. I figured that I knew something, at least a little, about suffering—that I knew people who had suffered. And when I worked at the factory, I'd been in some difficult situations, and I knew that those situations would always be harder than writing. I'm not saying that the anguish of writing is false. It is real for those who don't have a memory of true suffering. But when you have the memory of loss, or arriving in a city where you know no one, of being seen as the lowest of the low...

What do you remember of that time?

To watch someone see you, when you are begging or homeless, and the person isn't scandalized. He's not happy about it, but he is thinking that if someone has to be homeless, it might as well be you. If you say that someone you went to school with had become homeless, you would be scandalized. You would say to yourself, *It can't possibly be.* Yes, but for all the others who are homeless, it can't possibly be either. But it's like that when you don't know the person: you are categorized by race, or in a segment of society that we accept seeing in a miserable situation. Indigenous people drinking on a street corner or blacks in dire circumstances. These are things society thinks are normal. I'm not saying they accept it, but it's something they've always seen. Well, I've been in that situation, I've been seen that way. *He's an immigrant and not white, and he's in dire straits: that's normal.* There is nothing more extraordinary than seeing compassion in someone's eyes, but not the slightest surprise. At your situation. That is what it is to be a desert island. With no one to protect you. Which could plunge some people into despair, bordering on insanity. But for a writer, it can be interesting. Because you can observe society from that perspective, since you are completely invisible. No one sees you. You can watch things calmly. People will say and do anything in front of you. They see you as a Martian. People will speak as they wish in front of people who cannot transmit their message to others. I've been in that situation, where people spoke in front of me however they wanted.

Don't you find that the same thing happens now that people know you're a writer?

No—people *confide* in me now. It's the opposite: they speak to me so that I will write about it. There's a confessional quality to it. But it isn't freedom. It's the desire people have to be part of a book, to at least see their emotions attain the universal or the timeless. That's an intimacy that they share. They'll say true things, even hard things about themselves, but the agreement stipulates that they are doing so in order to transport their feelings into another era. It's like a message in a bottle;

for others to know how we lived. It's like a rocket to the moon: we put all our true thoughts into it, so that others will know us. Yes, people come to speak with me now, they come to find a place in the story for themselves. They would like what they've lived to enter the chain of memories. But that isn't the same thing as speaking freely.

You've also been able to write freely. In fact, you've been able to write some of your books in just a month.

Yes, often it only takes me a month—as with *Le charme des après-midis sans fin*. I don't experience any suffering in writing. It's like a second, alternate state.

The time of writing.

It isn't necessarily a joyous state. It's like living faster, or with greater intensity. I'm not at all wrapped up in what I'm going to write. I'm not scared when I can't write. I just don't write. I don't have that issue. I can extricate myself from the writing. But I really like it when I'm in that second state, where you are no longer just yourself, where you are inhabited. As they say in Vodou, you get mounted by the spirits, by emotions. You are several, not just you alone. Naturally, it requires a sort of self-expansion. You have to open space up. You can no longer live this life at the same time, you can no longer occupy yourself with all your normal concerns and petty obligations. You have to create space. You cannot enter into that generous nature, with all of its characters, in an excessively narrow space. You have to open the house up, make new rooms, guest rooms, to welcome everyone in. You can't put them all up in the same room. That's part of what can sometimes be hard. You have to forget about certain things that you would like to do. You have to make a choice. It's mainly hard for the people who live around you. Because all of a sudden you can no longer hear what they're saying to you. You cannot hear them.

Because you are in...

Because there are so many other people speaking to us. We're already deep in other conversations.

ACKNOWLEDGEMENTS

I wish to offer my heartfelt *remerciements* to Dany La-ferrière for his time and generosity, not to mention all the life-changing insights. Every moment spent with him, whether in person or in reading his work—or, especially, when working on these interviews—has been a deep pleasure. Although these conversations took place well before COVID-19, many of the brightest parts of this pandemic were, for me, those which involved *Working in the Bathtub*.

Thank you to Laura L. Taylor for her beautiful prints. At *The Paris Review*, thank you to Emily Nemens, Lorin Stein, Sadie Stein, Nicole Rudick, and Susannah Hunnewell, may she rest in peace. Thank you to everyone I am so fortunate to work with at the Wylie Agency: Jeffrey Posternak, Tracy Bohan, Jessica Calagione, Jessica Henderson, and Mia Vitale. Thank you to Sunny Doyle, who transcribed the interviews. (Any errors in the translations, or anywhere else between these covers, are mine alone.)

My endless gratitude to Michelle Sedell Szigeti, Maggie Berrouët, Camille Robitaille, Jennifer McMorran, Donald Antrim, Suroosh Alvi, Roger Tellier Craig, Sefi Amir, Jason Sanchez, Carlos Sanchez, Robbie Dillon, Lori Schubert and the QWF, Martino Gozzi and all my dear friends at Scuola Holden, Dean Chenoy, Jax Andison, David Gawley, Annie Briard, my brothers Michael and Julian, and my father András Göllner.

The biggest thank you of all goes to my dear mum, Linda Leith, a lifelong champion of literature in Montreal and beyond. She not only introduced me to Dany Laferrière ten years ago, she also inspired me to become a writer in the first place. It was a joy to collaborate with her on this book, which she has edited and published so lovingly.

—Adam Leith Gollner,
July 1, 2020

ACKNOWLEDGEMENTS

Linda Leith Publishing graciously acknowledges Dany Laferrière's invaluable contribution to this book.

—Linda Leith, President & Publisher,
July 1, 2020